THE VANILL.. ~~~..~~ ~

A SYSTEM

FOR

ASPIRING GALVANISERS EVERYWHERE

By

Sue Lownds

Pause For Space Publications

Pause for Space Publications

Lea Hall, Tunstall Lane, Bishops Offley, Eccleshall, ST21 6EU

Published by Pause for Space Publications, 2003

ISBN 0-9543662-1-2

For orders : please email:-

info@pauseforspacepublications.com

© Sue Lownds, 2003

Pause for Space Publications - we specialise in quick read books.

YOU ARE A GALVANISER
IF YOU HAVE THE APTITUDE AND THE APPETITE
FOR MAKING THINGS HAPPEN
AT ANY ORGANISATIONAL LEVEL.

THIS DOES NOT MEAN YOU HAVE
TO POSSESS A HUGE PUBLIC PERSONALITY.
YOU CAN FIRE UP PEOPLE IN DIFFERENT WAYS.
YOU CAN BE REFLECTIVE AND CONSIDERED,
BUT YOU DO HAVE TO MAINTAIN
GENUINE CONTACT WITH PEOPLE AT ALL LEVELS.

DEDICATION

As I write this book I am working with four different
groups of galvanisers who are grappling with the features of new
corporate philosophies that they find stretching to explain,
stimulating to sustain, messy to implement,
and motivating to watch unfolding.

This book is dedicated to them all.

They are an example of that special combination of the human gifts
of courage and experimentation, observation and interpretation,
patience and personal judgement that can exist in us all.

Special thanks to Ken, Rebecca, Nick, Anne, Stella and Michael for
their belief in The Vanilla Concept® from the start.
Thanks also to Hugh, Lindsay, Katharine and Paul for being curious
and experimental and supportive enough to join the earliest trial all
those years ago and to all my customers who have applied various
aspects of the system.

THE VANILLA CONCEPT

A SYSTEM FOR

ASPIRING GALVANISERS EVERYWHERE

To Zara
With best wishes
Sue Lownds

Sue Lownds has worked in the field of Human Resources and Organisational Development for twenty years in a wide range of sectors and organisations. She and her husband, Ken, live and run their consultancy business from a country base in Staffordshire, which serves both as a home and as a learning retreat for their customers. Sue is a Fellow of the Chartered Institute of Personnel and Development. She has written and spoken at seminars about the development of in house consultants to capitalise on the skill and will in organisations. The motto of The Vanilla Concept®, through which an organisation's own people are licensed to use her methodology, is 'Transferring Our Know-how To You'. Sue is a Classics graduate, a source of enjoyment and stimulation that had largely been supplanted by other interests until she found that her classical roots supplied a suitable way to highlight the qualities of the organisational influencers with whom she has worked, observed and researched for many years. (See the 'Author's Introductory Thoughts' for an explanation of the classical origins of The Vanilla Concept imagery).

References Acknowledgement

This book has been designed as a taster of The Vanilla Concept®. The exercises in this volume are the copyright of The Vanilla Concept® programme which is available under licence for in-house use.

Further details and information can be found at:-

www.thevanillaconcept.com

There are fourteen references to methodology, tools or techniques plus a number of case studies. They are sourced from the following Vanilla® development materials:-

Room to Master – a methodology for raising influencing performance at senior management level.

Room to Develop – for developing the influencing performance of team leaders, managers and potential managers.

Room to Excel – raising team performance.

Room to Breathe – managing personal aspirations.

For your convenience, the tools and techniques are summarised in a table at the end of this book on page 125.

CONTENTS

AUTHOR'S INTRODUCTORY THOUGHTS

I've had great pleasure putting this book together. Writing it was the suggestion of a customer, who saw The Vanilla Concept as offering three things to organisations:-

- Convenience – it's an easy-to-follow system,

- Productivity – it's about raising performance through sensible influencing,

- Value – its licensing system advocates the use of internal talent rather than external consultancy.

This volume is also about those so-called 'soft skills' that are not soft at all – they are the mobilising behaviours of business and they require guts, commitment, considered judgement and systematic application, exactly the kind of stuff of which galvanisers are made. I choose the word galvaniser because that is how I've been struck by the organisational women and men I have seen at all levels, influencing and motivating their people to higher and higher performance (you will meet some examples of their good practice in the case studies in these pages). They showed a knack for making the most of themselves and the most of the people around them, doing it, as they would say themselves, "without rocket science", finding a way to work with whatever the world had offered them.

Making the most of yourself and others is the focus of this book. If you are responsible for people in an organisation, you are a potential galvaniser. You will know that, for any business to deliver and keep delivering against its business plan, it is dangerous to rely only on the goodwill of people to plug the gaps in communication or to compensate for shortcomings in management behaviour. Continually adding to their team skills and interpersonal conduct as well as your own is critical to business delivery. The Vanilla Concept is a system for investing in both, and one which need not involve high expenditure if you are prepared to use the talent that, for sure, is all around you.

Since this volume has been designed as a quick read (perhaps for those commuter journeys) and a taster of the whole Vanilla system, I have responded to some of my customers who suggested the exercises, tools and techniques they have found most useful. My thanks to them. While it offers a galvaniser's *method*, The Vanilla Concept also employs a *creative* side, not least the title 'Vanilla', which is a mnemonic which forms the backdrop to the method.

So, why "vanilla"?

Because all the galvanisers I have met in organisations exhibit a pattern of interpersonal strengths that are the essence of their capacity to influence. "Vanilla" is a mnemonic that conveniently and creatively represents these essential qualities with images from Greek and Roman mythology. The galvaniser's system described in these pages stretches and reinforces every one of these qualities.

VULCAN - courage and innovation.

Vulcan, the Roman god of fire and spirit. He was also a creative craftsman. His Greek counterpart, Hephaestos, was depicted as lame, yet overcame his lameness through making the best, like all the galvanisers I have met, of his circumstances.

ATHENA - grounded common sense.

Athena, the goddess of wisdom. She was often depicted in armour, ready, like all galvanisers, for action and ready to apply her good sense, insights and learning to achieve her goals.

NEREUS - the capacity to put oneself in the shoes of others, seeing things as they do, the better to understand and influence them.

Nereus was a mythological old man of the sea. He possessed two important influencing attributes – (i) the gift of being able to become someone else – therefore, the capacity to see things from the point of view of another (including his opponents and competitors), and (ii) the magnanimity to give fair praise to (and to learn from) a competitor's or opponent's achievements.

ICARUS – the readiness to take a risk.

Icarus was the son of the great inventor Daedalus who, in Greek mythology, manufactured wings for man to fly. Icarus tested the wings and reminds us of two things – that a degree of risk taking is a quality of successful achievers, but that over-confident risk taking without listening to voices of experience is dangerous. (Icarus did not heed his father's advice, flew too near the sun and fell to his death when the wax in the wings melted).

LUDUS – Latin for 'game'.

The most successful influencers and galvanisers clearly communicate their game plan. They continuously revisit and fine-tune their game plan.

LAUREUS – the crown of laurels.

The crown of laurels was awarded to the winner of the ancient Olympic games. It represents the galvaniser's continuous investment in high standards.

APOLLO - the god of sun, light and clarity.

The sun god represents the capacity of galvanisers to simplify and clarify complexity for all to understand.

I have tried to cater for a variety of communication preferences in the way I have presented the information. So, in these pages, you will find structure, method and models for the 'authoritative' and 'considered' communicators, colour, imagery and narrative for the 'enthusiastic' communicator (see Chapter Two for the communication preferences). I hope you will find here aspects of The Vanilla Concept to suit your own circumstances and your own style.

Sue Lownds

THE GALVANISER'S SYSTEM

YOU CANNOT FIRE UP PEOPLE UNLESS
YOU CONNECT WITH THEM

YOU CANNOT CONNECT WITH THEM UNLESS
YOU KNOW AND UNDERSTAND THEM

YOU CANNOT UNDERSTAND THEM UNLESS
YOU ARE ABLE TO PUT YOURSELF IN THEIR SHOES

TO PUT YOURSELF IN THEIR SHOES YOU MAY NEED
TO COME OUT OF YOUR COMFORT ZONE

YOU MAY NEED TO CHANGE YOUR
METHOD OF COMMUNICATION

YOU MAY NEED TO SHARE YOUR THOUGHTS AND HOPES
AND TO BUILD RELATIONSHIPS
IN A WAY YOU ARE NOT USED TO DOING

THE GALVANISER'S SYSTEM AT A GLANCE

Each chapter will take you through a phase of this system, supplying techniques and approaches that a galvaniser could use to influence business performance (individual, team, self).

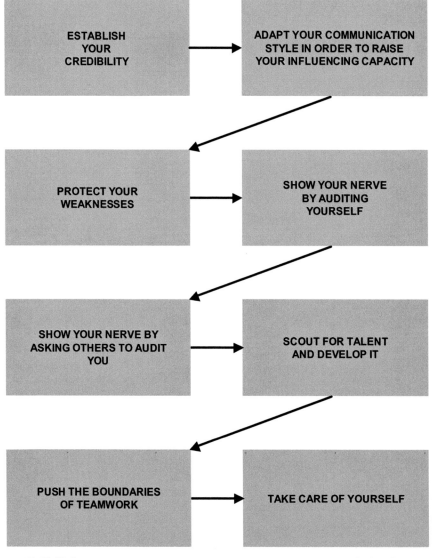

The Vanilla Concept   Sue Lownds

GALVANISERS ESTABLISH THEIR CREDIBILITY BY
LIVING THEIR FINE WORDS

CHAPTER ONE

CREDIBILITY ONLY REQUIRES
THE SIMPLEST AND MOST STRAIGHTFORWARD
OF CONNECTIONS - THE CONNECTION BETWEEN
WHAT WE SAY AND WHAT WE DO.
A MISMATCH BETWEEN WORDS AND BEHAVIOUR
BLOWS A HOLE IN OUR ABILITY
TO TAKE OTHERS WITH US.

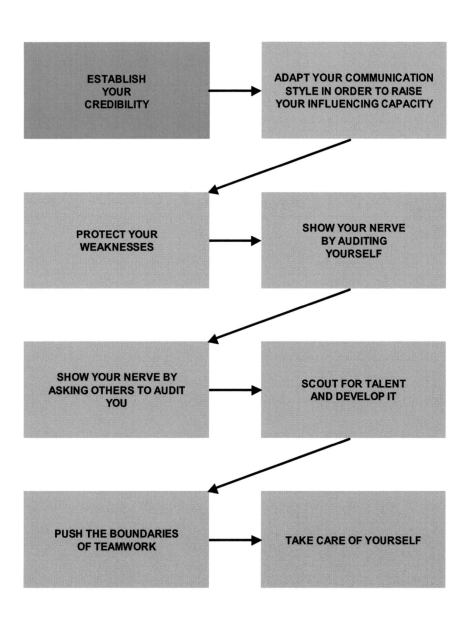

Chapter One Snapshot

The *street cred* of all galvanisers is determined by the extent to which their behaviour matches their words. To convince and motivate others they *invest systematically* in ensuring their actions match their words. This chapter supplies a role model's model (TL²) and case examples to show how two galvanisers lined up their words and behaviour.

Taking others with you is an element of interpersonal mastery. Interpersonal mastery is about connecting with people. You may be a terrific organiser, a masterful technician, an able financier. You may even have an ambitious vision for your organisation. If you cannot carry people with you, you are not a galvaniser. The capacity to galvanise others does not necessarily require inspirational oratory. It means that your behaviour is credible and engaging.

What will convince your people?

- They will expect to experience your clarity of thought and direction.

- They will expect to see a match between your words and your deeds. If there is a mismatch, they will not believe you. Credible behaviour includes owning up to mistakes – people will respect your honesty and your willingness to be challenged.

GALVANISERS ARE INFLUENCERS OF OTHERS,
CARRYING PEOPLE WITH THEM.
TL^2 IS A 'FIGURE OF EIGHT' MODEL FOR TAKING PEOPLE
WITH YOU, MOVING THROUGH 'THINK IT', 'TALK IT', 'LOVE
IT' AND FINALLY 'LIVE IT'.

Think It

Galvanisers start by :-

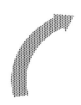

1. Working through the whole argument (e.g. What goal? Why? In what way will the change impact the organisation / my people / me? What do I actually have to *do?)*

2. Contingency planning ('What if?' scenarios e.g. What if I, personally, cannot deliver x, y, z?)

3. Personal Support (Where are my personal allies? Where and in whom will I be able to place most trust?)

Love It

Galvanisers demonstrate their total commitment by :-

1. Initiating activities that will reinforce the change or take it on another step (i.e. rather than reacting to the initiative of others).

2. Evaluating how they are doing.

Talk It

Galvanisers talk about the goal and encourage discussion.

1. Goals are stated in clear language.

2. Style is adjusted to meet differing communication needs (see Chapter Two).

3. Management meetings regularly include (a) progress checks on each person's personal contribution to the goal and (b) opportunities to discuss any personal support needed.

4. Willingness to discuss with, listen to, and learn from others.

Live It

Galvanisers line up their behaviour with their stated philosophy :-

1. Daily demonstration of the desired behaviour.

2. Active backing of those who support the process.

3. Not shirking opportunities to persuade and influence the cynics and resisters.

There are links, like the links of a chain, in the galvaniser's method. Galvanisers are the key to organisational transformation. Personal stocktaking is part of any process of transformation and is embedded in the method because galvanisers appreciate that bringing about change may require changes in themselves, too. Their prime influencing device is the credibility of their own behaviour – living it and, in a test of personal honesty, checking their own motives (i.e. revisiting the 'Think It' phase of the TL² model).

Some of the most impressive galvanisers, in recognising the reality of what they have to work with (their own human qualities), have had the security of character and strength of foresight to gather around them a collection of people to help them to close the gaps in their own capability (more of this in Chapter Three). So, examining one's conscience is no less than a sensible health check for the leaders of any movement for change. It's a time for no-kidding personal honesty.

"Example is not the main thing in influencing others, it is the only thing."
Albert Schweitzer

"What you are speaks so loudly, I can't hear what you say."
Ralph Waldo Emerson

Here are two examples of LIVE IT behaviour. Both the managers in these cases spoke eloquently and frequently about people being their organisation's greatest assets. We often hear such words in organisations. Living those words calls for a galvanising contact with people. The first case is a test of GENUINE CONTACT, the second an example of UNEXPECTED INVOLVEMENT.

A TEST OF GENUINE CONTACT

Use the case of Andrew J to compare it with the quality of your own contact. He provides four principles which he uses as a yardstick for what he calls "genuine, not political, contact".

AJ's FOUR-POINT YARDSTICK

"Contact is not about whether it takes place, but how often and how well," said Andrew J in his introduction to the organisation's newly devised management effectiveness training programme. "I'll give you four examples or principles of what I mean, and then we'll break into discussion groups to examine how, as managers carrying the responsibility for critical operational areas, we are going to achieve these things and live these principles."

PRINCIPLE 1.
There is no excuse for not knowing well all those who report to us directly and as many as possible in our total departments and functions.
If we don't know what makes people tick, we cannot make the most of them.

PRINCIPLE 2.

The expression "management controls" should be replaced by "manager controls".

We need to learn from the recipients of our style without letting power and authority get to our heads.

PRINCIPLE 3.

Every time I visit any part of the operation I make a point of seeking some new information about how my people view me.

This informal feedback is an invaluable temperature check on how effective we are.

PRINCIPLE 4.

If I disappeared tomorrow, there are at least six people I have personally developed who could step into my shoes.

If we do not coach, we are not fully effective managers.

Compare yourself, privately or in discussion with others, against Andrew's four principles. It is well worth taking the time to do this thoroughly. Operational life is such these days, that few of us take the time to take stock in this forthright way. Even if you are someone who cannot undertake all of this in one go, keep track of your progress as you keep dipping in. If this exercise is done in a group situation, you will probably find that the discussion will begin tentatively and gather pace and that the most productive areas will not be reached for some time. Small groups are most productive (e.g. four people).

UNEXPECTED INVOLVEMENT

Compare the two leadership approaches below and judge which is the more valuable contact for a galvaniser.

A particular Chief Executive made monthly visits to a major construction site where planned presentations were delivered for his information, where there was a general clean up and vases of flowers even appeared where none existed before.

He would have left with the kind of good news that makes good public relations reading and keeps the City feeling comfortable; he would have gleaned hardly anything at all about the real *human* dimension - what being involved in that project meant to the man putting up a thousand brackets, or to the storeman who had taken the plunge and run his first continuous improvement group, or to the electrician who left his family in the North of England at 3 am on Monday morning in order to be on site for his week's shift at 8 am.

His priorities were connected more with public relations, with photo opportunities and with the City and shareholder value than with the reality of working life for his people.

His approach is something of a contrast with another company director who, on being chauffeured around his organisation's various retail outlets during planned visits, would redirect the chauffeur unexpectedly to outlets that were not on the planned route and drop in without ceremony or announcement for an informal chat, lunch with the staff, or a conversation at someone's work station.

An extremely busy man with time for the people of his sizeable organisation because he understood that it is they, more than he, more than the shareholders, who actually delivered the business.

PAUSE FOR THOUGHT

How would you describe the *quality* of your contact with those you need to influence and motivate?

When, how and where do you find that you get most out of that contact? What makes the difference? How can you capitalise on that difference?

Do you know what others get out of their contact with you?

How can you make more of each influencing opportunity?

GALVANISERS ADAPT
THEIR STYLE OF COMMUNICATION
TO THEIR LISTENERS' NEEDS IN ORDER TO
RAISE THEIR INFLUENCING CAPACITY

CHAPTER TWO

IF YOU WANT TO INFLUENCE PEOPLE
YOU NEED TO SPEAK THEIR LANGUAGE, NOT YOURS

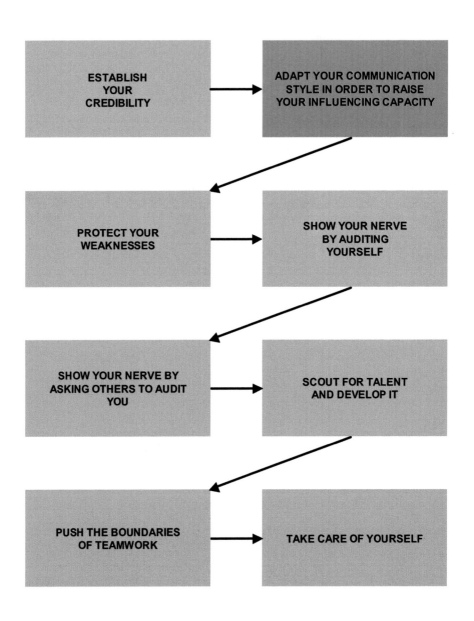

> ## Chapter Two Snapshot
>
> Tuning in to the communication preferences of those you are seeking to influence is a vital galvanising technique. This chapter introduces you to a method for reaching three differing communication styles. Galvanisers consistently cater for a range of communication needs in order to connect with people whose style is different from their own.

TL^2 is a model for galvanising conduct. But catchy models alone will not do it. Influencing others needs a thoughtful approach to communication - an adjustment of communication style to reach a variety of communication needs.

Here's a useful technique for influencers to help you to cater for different communication needs.

1.   The Authoritative Preference (a preference for structure, time management, results)

2.   The Considered Preference (a preference for data, reflection time, detail, method)

3.   The Enthusiastic Preference (a preference for the big picture, a focus on people, digression, anecdote)

If you only ever communicate in one style, you might only ever reach people with the same style as yourself. Using all three greatly increases your capacity to influence. Every time you communicate with an audience, there is likely to be a mixture of listening preferences. Offer each preference one or two elements of what appeals to it. The table on the next page shows you how.

The case study that follows is an example of how a thoughtful and simply-delivered communication strategy can sometimes better serve a business than overhauling its structures and processes.

A COMMUNICATOR'S SAFETY NET
CATERING FOR THREE DIFFERING COMMUNICATION NEEDS

THE AUTHORITATIVE COMMUNICATION PREFERENCE	THE CONSIDERED COMMUNICATION PREFERENCE	THE ENTHUSIASTIC COMMUNICATION PREFERENCE
To reach people with this preference, give your communication:- • a strong and obvious structure • a pacey delivery • clear business outcomes • rigorous time management and regular time checks • clarity of purpose • regular, succinct summaries • an agenda in advance	To reach people with this preference, give your communication:- • an emphasis on facts, figures, data, including graphs and diagrams • an emphasis on past track record • an emphasis on method and system • reflection time • written reference information • an agenda in advance	To reach people with this preference, give your communication:- • an emphasis on the big picture • concepts more than data • a consideration of the impact on people • imagination • an exploration of ideas, especially new ideas • an opportunity for involvement

TAILORING AND TUNING IN

Rebecca's Communication Experience

Rebecca is an experienced Finance Manager in a plastics production plant. She was voted Chair of a project team that was tasked with producing recommendations for increasing cross-organisational and cross-operational cooperation in an organisation that 'sold' itself as a business that highly valued its customers, yet had slid into operating within structures and conventions that delivered slow and often inaccurate responses to customer queries. The project team was encouraged to look at organisational structure, procedures and training.

Rebecca's project colleagues included ten managers from different functions - Customer Services, Production, Marketing, Strategy, Distribution and Human Resources. Rebecca was inexperienced as a project manager, but had been voted into the Chair's role by her colleagues because they saw her as an effective team worker.

Rebecca explains the situation her team faced.

"We knew we had a challenge on our hands. Customer surveys over the past fifteen months had shown increasing levels of customer frustration. Our compensation records revealed an increase in customer compensation arrangements. Staff surveys over the same period indicated high levels of stress caused by poor information, poor levels of coordination and cooperation. When we checked staff survey results with our absence statistics, we found that absence levels had increased over the past year by a staggering 30%. Much of this absence was in the very areas which were most important to customer contact – in the service centre, in the warehouse and in transport. The cost was not just time, but efficiency and productivity and morale – and future customers, if our depleting reputation became a talking point in the industry. Our business depended on finding an early solution to our internal mismanagement. We realised that a lot rested on our performance as a project team and on me. I knew I faced a steep learning curve but I was stimulated by the prospect of making a difference. The biggest learning of all proved to be that the solution rested not in a major overhaul of company structures, as many had expected, but in something much more simple and human."

The early stages of the project team's work together proved difficult, with vested interests and protectionism showing themselves to a degree even within the team. Rebecca admits to being worried that they would never deliver a satisfactory solution within the deadlines that had been set for them. She had found that a feature of project meetings was the revisiting of point after point for further clarification.

"What brought it home to me was our fourth meeting when Dorothy, who worked in the warehouse, said 'Sometimes I just don't think we are speaking the same language. We're supposed to be on the same side in this project team and if we can't make sense of each others' points what is it like out there?' I began to realise that, maybe under my influence, our communication was stressing figures and data, rather than what was behind the data. So I reminded the group of the amount of time we had spent going over the same or similar ground and I asked each of them to tell me honestly how they wanted information presented to them – what would make most sense to them, what would be easy for them to work with. I don't know why I hadn't thought of this before. We started to support each statistic with examples of the actual behaviours and situations that contributed to it and the picture began to make sense to us all."

When the team began to look at the behaviours that were unhelpful in delivering service, they began to realise that they, too, exhibited some of those behaviours - an example of the depth of the culture of separation from the customer and from each other. Here are some of the examples they unearthed:-

- People would walk past a ringing telephone so as to avoid being "caught up" in a situation that was outside their own area.

- Customers complained of the numbers of times people would say "I can't help you", "You'll have to speak to X and she is at lunch at the moment", "Can you call back later?". The irritators were "I can't help you", "You'll *have* to…" , "Can *you* call back…?"

- Lack of ownership resulted from the fact that many people simply did not appreciate their personal contribution to the whole business and did not see how their behaviour could possibly affect the bottom line.

- Front line staff – such as drivers who met customers daily or warehouse staff who took telephone calls from customers regarding delivery arrangements – had come to look upon themselves as "operatives" rather than as customer service contacts. No training or support had been given to them on handling their customer contacts – they did their best but, in making excuses, often made the situation worse by passing the blame on to other departments.

- Information requested by "operatives" was rarely delivered promptly – they were unimportant in the hierarchy.

The project team concluded that the one action that would make the most immediate difference would be the raising of awareness of each person's individual business contribution. They decided to test this out.

Learning from their own experience of miscommunication, the team chose to invest effort and good sense in the best form of communication. They chose three areas for their test - one of the production shifts, the mixing plant, and the drivers.

They worked with the people in each of the test areas:-

- to determine what they already knew about the workings of the business, the range and value of the customer base and how their own work helped the business to make money,

- to establish the aspects of the business that were not fully understood or were misunderstood,

- to understand how people acquired this information,

- to compare the acquisition of business knowledge with the acquisition of operational knowledge.

They discovered six significant points:-

1. Operational know-how was generally high and this was acquired through a combination of formal induction and daily fifteen-minute briefings at the start of each working day.

2. Business knowledge, on the other hand, was acquired in disjointed pieces and from no one source.

3. People had very little knowledge of the value of each customer to the business.

4. People tended to see customer service as being someone else's area of responsibility, rather than part of their own.

5. They had no appreciation at all of how significant they were to the customer and to the business bottom line.

6. They valued and strongly backed their own colleagues but felt little connection with the rest of the organisation.

With the agreement of shift supervisors, team leaders and managers, the morning briefings were extended by fifteen minutes. This extra time was used to describe the strong and essential links between each section's operational work and the money the business made – for example, how much a driver's delivery was worth to the organisation, how much difference the speed of production made to the bottom line, what precise costs could be incurred by an error in the mixing plant, what was the financial, production and human impact of a Health and Safety error.

Team leaders were given advance information in order to deliver these briefings. In addition, they were supported at each meeting by a member of Rebecca's project team, who answered questions and gave more information if necessary. Rebecca explains the care they took to meet the communication needs of their listeners.

"One really important aspect of this was to connect with our test group. They objected to anything that sounded to them like "management speak" but they responded to very precise, practical connections between the work they were doing and what the customers said they wanted.

"We found ourselves speaking almost in bullet points – very short sentences, very practical content, very direct information about costs. We talked of money made, not profits. We talked of customer reactions, not feedback. We talked of problem solving not query resolution. We talked about how much money each shift produced. These may sound like terribly simple things, but we found they mattered.

"Within one week, people began talking about the cost and value of each shift, the cost and value of each mixing batch, and the value and potential value of each customer. We had hit on the simplest of ways to engage people.

"Another aspect that proved very important, to judge from the customer response, was the change in the way drivers handled customers at the point of delivery. When faced with a customer request or a problem, they immediately set about trying to deal with it on the spot. In the past they would have brought it back to base, losing valuable time and leaving a less than satisfied customer.

"To overcome their reluctance to take on this role, we agreed that Catherine (the Customer Services manager on the project team) would accompany each driver on three deliveries. They would use the driving time to talk about the customer whose delivery they were about to make and, using the driver's past experience, to anticipate any possible issues *and* the way the customer liked them handled.

"This seems so obvious now – we were simply tapping the knowledge in people's heads to deliver an effective service. There seemed to be an assumption at the start of the project that we had problems of organisational structure that needed to be addressed. In the end, we probably saved a whole lot of money and aggravation by re-communicating, not restructuring."

By the time the project team reported back to senior management, they had more than recommendations. They had the first results of their tests. They also had their own learning to share. They were able to extrapolate from that learning, communication recommendations for the rest of the organisation.

- They showed that gaps in knowledge could fairly easily be filled if the right communication *relationship*, as well as *method*, was used.

- They produced data on the amount of time they had saved within the project team by altering the way they communicated with each other.

- They demonstrated that, if information was communicated in the way that suited the receiver, rather than the deliverer, people could readily be motivated to identify with and take ownership of the business.

- They produced first evidence of the positive reactions of customers to the drivers' speedier response to their needs.

- They produced first evidence of the growing cohesion within the organisation upon which closer working could now be built.

- They showed that a business need not respond to problems by changing its structure if the most straightforward of human skills and good sense are applied with a cool head.

Rebecca's project team had moved forward, not just in influencing each other and their selected test areas through adjusting its communication, but also in influencing the 'authoritative' members of senior management (see the communications table on page fifteen) who responded positively to the emphasis on results and action.

PAUSE FOR THOUGHT

Think back over situations where you have struggled to influence others. To what extent do you think that adjusting your *style* of communication might have made a difference in helping your listeners to connect with you?

GALVANISERS PROTECT
THEIR WEAKNESSES

CHAPTER THREE

YOU MAY NOT BE INSPIRATIONAL ALL OF THE TIME,
BUT YOU CAN USE THE TALENT AROUND YOU,
WISELY AND HONESTLY,
TO MAKE IT EASIER ON YOURSELF
TO GALVANISE OTHERS.

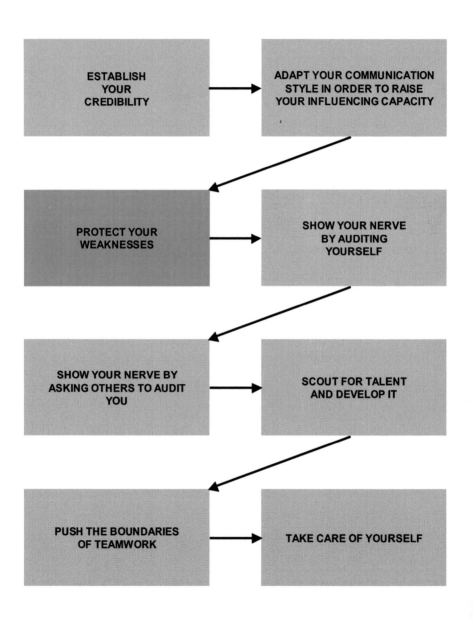

Mobilising people requires a combination of talent AND inclination. You may not possess all the necessary influencing skills and qualities, but others around you probably have some that you do not have.

You can employ a system of surrounding yourself with a number of *Dedicated Ambassadors*, chosen for skills, qualities and know-how that complement your own. This requires a degree of self-criticism and self-knowledge on your part.

Your position or status may lead others to view you as the prime mover and meeting their expectations may place strains on you if you do not possess the full range of capability.

Mull over the *Prime Mover* qualities on the page 29. Do you possess them in abundance? Look around you. Your potential allies are all around and you could use them, without making a big deal of it, as your own *Dedicated Ambassadors*.

- A Prime Mover is a person who initiates change.

- Dedicated Ambassadors are those who can be called upon to back up the Prime Mover and whose skills and qualities fill the gaps in the Prime Mover's own capability.

"On the strength of one link in the cable
Dependeth the might of the chain"

Admiral Ronald A Hopwood – The Laws of the Navy

DISTINGUISHING CHARACTERISTICS OF THE PRIME MOVER

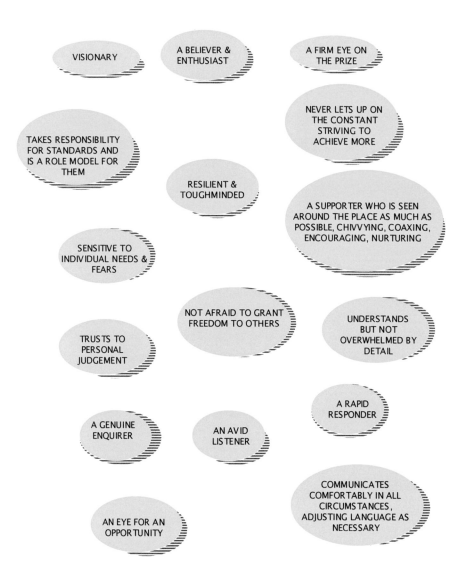

VISIONARY

A BELIEVER & ENTHUSIAST

A FIRM EYE ON THE PRIZE

NEVER LETS UP ON THE CONSTANT STRIVING TO ACHIEVE MORE

TAKES RESPONSIBILITY FOR STANDARDS AND IS A ROLE MODEL FOR THEM

RESILIENT & TOUGHMINDED

A SUPPORTER WHO IS SEEN AROUND THE PLACE AS MUCH AS POSSIBLE, CHIVVYING, COAXING, ENCOURAGING, NURTURING

SENSITIVE TO INDIVIDUAL NEEDS & FEARS

NOT AFRAID TO GRANT FREEDOM TO OTHERS

UNDERSTANDS BUT NOT OVERWHELMED BY DETAIL

TRUSTS TO PERSONAL JUDGEMENT

A RAPID RESPONDER

A GENUINE ENQUIRER

AN AVID LISTENER

COMMUNICATES COMFORTABLY IN ALL CIRCUMSTANCES, ADJUSTING LANGUAGE AS NECESSARY

AN EYE FOR AN OPPORTUNITY

THE PRIME MOVER AND THE DEDICATED AMBASSADOR

The story of Jacob in his own words

"I've never been a great orator – in fact I'd say it's a real weakness of mine. But I am a good networker and I'm certainly a spotter of talent.

"We had a big change of structure last year – high risk because people were already cynical about previous change and I knew that being able to reach them would make all the difference to keeping up our productivity during a time of difficult change. The trouble was that we were very short of time. I'd have much preferred to go around painstakingly talking to every small group in turn, but knew this was not achievable in the timescales.

"Joan was the head of Marketing and an inspiring and believable speaker to large groups. Between us we devised a system of informing and supporting people – large group announcements by Joan with her penchant for a sound argument and passionate belief in the future, and personalised support from me and a specially-selected team that I personally briefed and coached. Two different communication tactics employed with organisation, common sense and speed."

You may be a prime mover in one context and a dedicated ambassador in another. Self-awareness and self-honesty will determine when and how. The table below offers a few examples, taken from people in a number of different organisations and situations who combined strengths to compensate for weaknesses and to beef up personal and collective capability.

PRIME MOVER	DEDICATED AMBASSADOR
Organising Skills	Analytical Skills
Speed in absorbing information	Building relationships with people
Coaching talent	Decision-making skills
Oratory	Facilitation skills
Conceptual thinking	Factual thinking
Eagle's eye perspective	Worm's eye perspective
Task emphasis	Human emphasis
Focus on the present, the past	Focus on future possibilities
Innovation, Imagination	Realism
Preference for talking things through	Preference for thinking things through
Ability to see patterns in information that is presented	Systematic use of information
Preference for structure and boundaries	Preference for change
Numerical aptitude	Verbal aptitude

So, a person with conceptual thinking ability may team up where necessary with someone who is inclined to focus on facts, or someone with a strong numerical aptitude but a weak verbal aptitude could connect up with someone with the opposite capability.

Think about how and why some of the pairings of style and personal preference in the table may have been helpful in meeting the demands of organisational life. Bear in mind the discipline and adaptability that may be needed. In some of these examples (e.g. the alliance between the people of imagination and their down-to-earth colleagues), a considerable personal adjustment was needed to make the alliance work.

PAUSE FOR THOUGHT

Do you make it hard on yourself by trying to be everything to everyone?

To what extent do you look around you for those whose capability can beef up your own?

Take a look at the best influencers you know. How often can you see them using others to compensate for areas where they are less strong or less confident?

If you are about to undertake an assignment that will test you, how can you make alliances with others to cover your downside?

GALVANISERS DEMONSTRATE NERVE
BY IMPLEMENTING A SYSTEM OF SELF-AUDIT

CHAPTER FOUR

IF WE HIDE OUR HEADS IN THE SAND,
SOONER OR LATER WE'LL END UP SUFFOCATING,
OR ELSE WE WON'T BE ABLE TO SEE
WHAT'S ABOUT TO BITE US ON THE BEHIND.
TO STAY IN TOUCH WITH OUR OWN CAPABILITY,
WE NEED SYSTEMATICALLY TO ANALYSE
WHAT WE DO AND HOW WE DO IT,
EVEN IF IT THROWS UP SOME PAINFUL TRUTHS.
THIS IS NOT NAVEL GAZING BUT
A SENSIBLE HEALTH CHECK

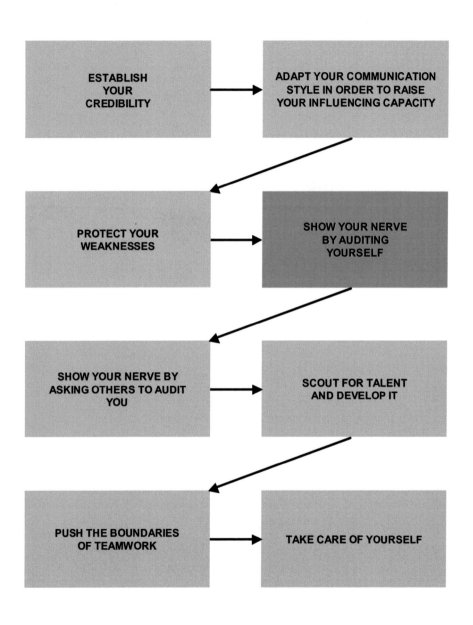

Chapter Four Snapshot

A strong feature of all galvanisers is nerve – nerve in assessing their own performance as well as that of others.

This chapter describes a system of self-audit called *The Three Leadership Calibres* through which galvanisers can demonstrate their capacity for (i) motivating others, (ii) managing performance and (iii) preparing people for the future.

The case study that follows is an example of how one leader put all three into practice, sometimes turning convention on its head in order to galvanise his organisation.

Galvanisers know that there are only three real duties for anyone who has responsibility for others – every other task, duty or aspiration fits into them. They are:-

1.   MOTIVATING PEOPLE SO THAT THEY PERFORM EFFECTIVELY.

2.   MANAGING AND MONITORING THEM WHILE THEY PERFORM.

3.   PREPARING THEM FOR THE FUTURE IN ORDER TO SAFEGUARD THE BUSINESS.

Take a look at the three circles below – *The Three Leadership Calibres*. Galvanisers audit themselves against these three calibres. They ask themselves a number of questions related to these calibres – questions like those listed on the next page. In the case study that follows, you will meet a man who put the three calibres into practice.

THE THREE LEADERSHIP CALIBRES

THE INSPIRATIONAL CALIBRE
(MOBILISING PERFORMANCE)

THE HEROIC CALIBRE
(MANAGING PERFORMANCE)

THE DEVELOPMENTAL CALIBRE
(LAYING THE FOUNDATIONS
FOR FUTURE PERFORMANCE)

QUESTIONS TO POSE TO YOURSELF
AGAINST THE THREE LEADERSHIP CALIBRES

THE INSPIRATIONAL CALIBRE (mobilising performance)

- What is the quality, nature and extent of my personal contact with my people?
- How can I improve it?

THE HEROIC CALIBRE (managing performance)

- To what extent do I have my finger on performance data?
- To what extent do I know and understand the human issues behind the data?
- How can I improve things?

THE DEVELOPMENTAL CALIBRE (laying the foundations for future performance)

- To what extent do I understand coming business challenges?
- How can I better ensure my people are ready for them?

THE PEOPLE PROJECT
THE THREE LEADERSHIP CALIBRES IN ACTION

"We are about to start doing what isn't the done thing around here and we are going to keep doing it until it becomes the way we do things around here."

The words of Geoff Clarke in one of his first speeches to the people in his business on becoming its Chief Executive. Geoff's words were followed by swift action, designed to shift organisational culture from, as he put it, "waiting for instructions and working in comfortable habits, to responsiveness to changing business needs, decisiveness in resolving business problems, and courage, innovation and determination in building successful teams."

Geoff chose three cultural and leadership areas to address:-

- The first was an investment in the role-modelling behaviour of the Top Team

- The second was a programme across the organisation, called Developing Successful Teams

- The third was a system of Workplace Coaching to replace most classroom training.

Geoff describes the business environment he came into.

"Technically skilled with a high investment in technology and proud of it. A pretty hierarchical mentality prevailed. Tension between management and unions existed. People embraced words like 'leadership' and 'teamwork' because it was not respectable not to. I found a severe mismatch between the words and the conduct. Training was bought in. A high value was (and still is) put on operational capability, without fully appreciating that operational capability depends largely on the workability of teams and the workability of teams depends on all those human qualities, aptitudes and instincts that technology cannot deliver.

"I do think, though, that I've come into an environment of tremendous opportunity. That's my challenge. Incomers into an organisation often disparage the standards they see. I've seen that happen time and time again. But, for me, it's critical to preserve the best of the past because that's the foundation for the future. It's a balance between valuing what this organisation is (long - serving staff with enormous and irreplaceable organisational knowledge and a sense of history, sitting alongside [and often corrupted by] the attitudes of the rut), and a drive towards future opportunities which will only be achieved if the whole organisation learns to move more quickly."

I.   THE TOP TEAM

Geoff decided to capitalise on the culture of stability. He started at the top. Recognising that the Board had worked together in some cases for twenty years, he invested first in the top team *as a team*. This was new territory for his Board. In his first month he set up the first of regular Board team events. The purpose was not to discuss operational or corporate issues, but to work on themselves.

Before the first event, the Board members were given a shoe box and asked to fill it with items (business or personal) that were important to them. They would be asked to talk through these items. At the second and subsequent events, they developed the art of openly-delivered feedback. They were also invited to talk about what would happen to the business if one or more of them suddenly departed and who, in their team, they would choose to step into their shoes and why. Later events began to work in detail on specific aspects of the role of Board members – for example, their 'representation' of the business through internal and external presentations, an aptitude that was lacking in some.

Geoff describes the reactions.

"It was, I suppose, risky stuff - a long way from the customary technical and operational issues. This had been a business where, although a training programme existed, there was a sense that the people issues did not need close attention, that they would happen, somehow, when they needed to. There was no succession planning worth the title. Such was the task emphasis, that no one had ever taken the time to consider the costs to the business of poor people management, or the advances in productivity that could be gained from a focused investment in communication skills. I decided that the culture of hierarchy would work in my favour, and my status in the organisation worked for me. I am quite sure there were muted mutterings and many silent misgivings behind my back. Though I was testing human and communication aptitude, I chose not to tamper with work that had been done, before my arrival, on leadership competencies. The Board had approved these, I was told, so my goal was to ensure we all lived the words. Certainly there was a high degree of discomfort. I was trying to prove that the words the leaders of this organisation had chosen to express organisational values (words put together by them before my time) had to be acted out at leadership level for our people to see – otherwise they were meaningless. So, the words 'openness', 'trust' and 'teamwork' needed to be for real.

"I decided to force the issue. The results were more than I'd hoped for. We gained some valuable and personal insights into each other. I tended to lead off with the input because I wanted to set a certain standard of sharing. This doesn't mean that everyone offered revelations. Some people are very private. We allowed each person to say what he chose. What helped here were the long associations and base of loyalty and belonging to the company. People basically cared – they cared about the organisation and they cared about their contribution. They were also used to reading their leader and following his desires. Now that leader was me. I decided to work that culture in order to move the whole group on".

Geoff facilitated the first three events himself. Then, instead of bringing in an external consultant, Geoff invited an internal facilitator to work with the Board. This was another considered risk, taken to demonstrate openness. Prior to the event he spent personal time with each Board member, talking through how the event would work. The internal facilitator was four grades below board level. She was known to them all. Geoff gave his colleagues the opportunity to nominate others. They did not, saying they were happy with his choice.

The investment in the top team and Geoff's close involvement led directly to the next two phases of his "people project". All the directors led their own reportees in a set of events based on the top team events. Geoff made it known that he would expect to be invited along to some of them – and, true to form, the directors all obliged. His presence served two prime purposes – visible support and monitoring. The monitoring role enabled him to check on the actions of his top team and also to scout for future talent. ("A vital aspect of leadership in my view – to be ready for the future, you absolutely have to have the right people. Sometimes this is critical enough to take a personal hand in.").

II.   DEVELOPING SUCCESSFUL TEAMS

"For an organisation to be flexible enough to adapt to a rapidly changing business world and an ever more competitive future, we need people who have, not just the technical capability, and who are not just skilled and excellent at an individual level, but who are also skilled and excellent at a team level. For us, this means that we need people who can operate at an advanced interpersonal level in *any* team, because we are going to have constantly to reshape ourselves to meet the future and one of the great productivity setbacks is when new teams are formed. Speeding up this formation process is critical to our survival in a fast moving environment."

To achieve his advanced teams, Geoff commissioned three investments, which involved, among others, union members and representatives.

> *1. Every division had trained facilitators*

> *2. There was an investment in the productivity of meetings*

> *3. Each Team was granted restocking days.*

1.   Every division had trained facilitators

Facilitators received a small monetary reward.   Geoff posted an invitation on the intranet explaining that facilitators would be expected to contribute to the building of a strong team culture throughout the organisation.   Individuals were invited to put themselves forward for the role and to produce a paragraph on the intranet to say why they were interested and how they could contribute to the business.   Their own colleagues voted for the successful candidates.   This approach to a critical appointment was openly welcomed by some but disparaged by others more accustomed to the 'tap on the shoulder' mechanism of the past.

Facilitators came from a variety of levels.   They received concentrated training and then began to hold team-building days, to work with groups on decision-making and problem-solving, and to develop the art of feedback.   Behind their activities, as Geoff often reminded them, was the goal of early tackling of interpersonal issues that might impede the business effectiveness of the team.   "If people are spending their time covering their backs because they are afraid of blame, or bad mouthing their manager, or failing to pass on information promptly, the efficiency of the whole organisation suffers.   Our entire efficiency depends on speed of communication and high responsiveness."

Geoff began to invite facilitators to ad hoc and unplanned meetings with himself from time to time, dipping into their experiences as a progress barometer (in addition to feedback from his senior managers and his own visits around the organisation).   The facilitators soon began to be ready for these unscheduled invitations, ensuring they had ready the kind of information about achievements, outcomes and outstanding issues that they came to learn Geoff would require. One of his favourite questions to them became "And what would you say is the business impact of....?".

These monitoring sessions ensured not only that team development did not fall by the wayside but also that senior managers maintained a watchful eye on what was going on so that they, too, could respond with knowledge to Geoff's inevitable interest. There were some negative reactions to his connection with the facilitators, bypassing as it did conventional hierarchy. Some facilitators objected to being called "Geoff's clique" by their colleagues.

2.   *Meetings investment to improve productivity*

"Our managers are spending more than half their time in meetings," Geoff said during one of his bi-monthly visits around the patch. "If we calculated what that means in time and lost opportunity elsewhere, we'd be appalled. This is a costly culture. Part of it is due to poor meetings control, part of it is a comfortable routine of going round the same issues without making a decision". The hierarchical traditions of the organisation resulted in a grapevine instruction - "Geoff doesn't want us to hold meetings".

When the pendulum began to swing to the point that significant meetings were not held because of this imagined instruction, Geoff decided to challenge his senior managers to rework the meetings syndrome. He sought feedback on his own effectiveness as a chair and this became the custom after every board meeting.

Feedback included comments on:-

- the value of pre-meeting information,

- the clarity of the objective and the agenda,

- whether any item could have been better resolved without the meeting,

- time spent on individual agenda items,

- the speed of decisions.

He pushed them to offer areas for improvement and sought feedback when he acted on their suggestions. He rotated the role of chair so that every board member received similar feedback from their colleagues and from him.

He invited every director to ensure that these checks became a routine part of the meetings in their division and to report back to him at every third board meeting on their judgement of the productivity of the meetings in their division.

Over six months, the time spent on meetings was reduced by half. Some 35% of routine meetings stopped altogether when analysis showed that they were comfortable and enjoyable talking shops with no results. Instead, some of the team events were used as free-flowing, get-to-know-each-other sessions, leaving the focus of operational meetings on rigorous business outcomes.

3.   *Restocking days for every team, to use as they chose.*

Restocking days became an accepted part of team life, and represented a major change from an era where working away from the regular workplace was viewed as a skive, despite "Trust" being one of the stated values of the organisation. Each Director's division was allocated twenty restocking days per year. A budget was allocated for these days. Unused restocking days were not transferable to the following year. Restocking days could be used:-

- to allow individuals to work from home for specific reasons,

- for team strategy events,

- for team development,

- as a team or individual reward.

Their purpose was to recharge and reinvigorate individuals or groups by allowing them time outside the regular work environment. It was the responsibility of the teams to organise their workload to cater for these restocking days, covering for each others' work if necessary. Each director was asked to offer a half year account to his colleagues of how his restocking days were used. These served as a check as well as an opportunity to transfer learning and ideas.

The role of team facilitators included surveys of opinions on how these restocking days were working and how they could be better used. Opinion was generally positive, except where it was felt that certain individuals were granted special favours. The surveys themselves were positively received because opinions, however critical, were accepted and individuals were always asked to follow a criticism with a suggestion for improvement.

Geoff commented to his Board, "I want people to get used to not getting away with a criticism that is unsupported by example and is unsupported by at least one suggestion for improvement. Otherwise, we are still operating in that 'wait to be told' environment that I found when I arrived."

III.   WORKPLACE COACHING REPLACED CLASSROOM TRAINING

This was the element of change that proved most difficult to implement and required persistent encouragement from the directors. Workplace coaching required several attitudes:-

- high flexibility,

- openness and honesty,

- readiness to respond to a coach's observations,

- a readiness to innovate.

Classroom behavioural training had proved expensive and of limited effect. Perhaps because of the lack of monitoring after the training, transfer of learned behaviours was limited and appeared to rely on individual gumption alone. There was little attempt on the part of managers to engage with those attending training courses in order to brief or prepare them, or to motivate them, or to check up on their learning, or to help ensure that learning was transferred to the workplace.

A system of workplace coaching began to replace many of the classroom events. Workplace coaching was defined as "a bit by bit, day by day process of development, in the real work environment, supporting positive attitudes and behaviour and challenging unhelpful attitudes and behaviour without the need to take people out of the operation".

Geoff explains why.

"This is all about the motivation of our people. If they are not motivated, we all fail. The business fails. We have mountains of individual capability. It is not that we lack capable individuals. What we lacked was corporate capitalisation of individual talent. We suffered from this image of soft skills being pink and fluffy and non-operational. Not so, they are fundamental to the operation. We also suffered from this damned hierarchy.

"People talked of twenty years' experience. What I came across quite often, was one year's experience twenty times over. Until those at the top start taking a real interest in the issues of conduct that make a working environment motivational and start valuing that, we are always going to have a situation of piecemeal, and therefore limited transfer, from the classroom to the workplace.

"Classroom training is also expensive in valuable time. If it isn't the best way to change behaviour, then let's stop it and do something more effective."

Workplace coaching involved:-

- Managers identifying those whose behaviours most closely matched the behavioural competencies the organisation had devised and then done little with. These included, among others, such elements as:-

  o **Cooperation**

  o **Giving a bit extra**

  o **An innovative attitude to resolving problems**

- Talented people were invited to a 'masterclass' led by Geoff and his directors where the philosophy and business benefits of behavioural coaching were discussed and where individuals had a go at a number of exercises to demonstrate and develop the nature of workplace coaching. Together they whittled down eleven behavioural competencies to the three identified above – **cooperation** (defined as critical to operating as one team, rather than as several disparate sections), **giving a bit extra** (defined as critical to outdoing the competition) and **an innovative attitude to resolving problems** (defined as critical to a fast moving business environment).

In addition, the coaches suggested that workplace computer training would be more helpful than the standardised training packages that had been on offer. It was suggested that computer training needed to be meaningfully targeted to people's actual job needs. It was felt that the fact that some people would not have full and complete computer capability would be mitigated by higher operational effectiveness in the areas that were relevant. For an organisation that valued high technical competence, this was a marked change of emphasis.

- Commissioned by the directors, workplace coaches began to work in their own business environments to help their colleagues to develop themselves against the three behavioural competencies. The system relied on the gumption and resilience of the individual coaches as well as on the constant support and encouragement of the directors. It worked better in some areas than others. Geoff used his interest to keep pressure on those directors who were inclined to let this slip.

He did this in two ways:-

- In conjunction with coaches, Geoff and the directors took the right to delve into appraisals to track the attention paid in them to the behavioural competencies. Once this became known, there was a rush of managers seeking help in the completion and conduct of appraisals (this despite a former major investment in appraisal training). Team facilitators were there to help them.

- At quarterly forecast meetings, managers were required to talk about their people and to demonstrate that they were knowledgeable not just about their operational duties, but about what turned them on and off, about their aspirations and their personal development.

"There has been much faltering and the need for much support, but I think we are now seeing a shift in emphasis and a higher understanding and expectation of the business consequence of strong people management and leadership. I want managers to understand that, if we are known as an organisation that develops its people, their own life becomes easier because excellent people will carve a path to their door. We are considering altering the format of next year's staff survey from an anonymous, written process to a series of open discussions."

GEOFF'S SUMMARY OF THE IMPACT OF HIS 'PEOPLE PROJECT' AFTER THREE YEARS – (i) THE BENEFITS AND (ii) THE INVESTMENT.

(i) The Benefits

On the business	On Team Capability	On Individuals
• Faster moving • Less time spent on unnecessary meetings • A Board that is far more open, with problems more likely to be nipped in the bud • Training and development costs are better targeted • A better idea of individual capability to apply to succession • Greater and quicker response to change • A stronger match between leadership words and deeds – we are nearer being role models than ever before • More cohesion with union representatives	• High flexibility – we now have speedier responses to changing business demands. For example, when we reform teams, the speed with which teams are productive is impressive • Rapid problem solving, due in part to the investment in team facilitators who have ensured that a problem solving process has become part of the everyday culture • Performance data is readily available. I and the Board can now ask for information on team performance which is produced immediately. It used to take weeks.	• Motivation – as demonstrated by our annual staff surveys • Confidence – last month we had the highest number ever of suggestions in the staff suggestion scheme • Flexibility – people are ready to move around different teams. This is a major achievement from the old habits and comfortable rituals of the past. • Succession – we have identified and have started formally to develop talented people for the future • Time – people are freely giving of their time, putting in extra effort not just into their own development but into organisational projects

GEOFF'S SUMMARY OF THE IMPACT OF HIS 'PEOPLE PROJECT' AFTER THREE YEARS – (i) THE BENEFITS AND (ii) THE INVESTMENT.

(ii) The Investment

On the business	On Team Capability	On Individuals
• Senior management time • Development costs (e.g. facilitators and workplace coaches) • Settling down costs – for example, the hiccups, which did affect our productivity temporarily, over the misunderstanding about what I meant about the effectiveness of meetings	• Management time • Development costs (facilitators, team restocking days) • The human cost (also applicable to 'Business' and 'Individuals') of 10% staff turnover p.a. from 3% as people departed (mostly by necessity), whose performance was substandard	• Management time • Individual time • Development costs • Managing expectations (many are called but few will be chosen)

Geoff's 'People Project' is an example of the implementation of the three leadership calibres – a man who tested his leadership ability and found his own way of inspiring and motivating others (the inspirational calibre), of managing performance (the heroic calibre) and developing the people of his organisation (the developmental calibre), taking several risks and introducing innovations along the way.

Testing and auditing yourself against the three calibres may reveal areas for your own development and one way to address those areas for development is to self-coach. One of the extraordinary features of the galvanisers I have met is the way they *self-coach*. Self-coaching is an invaluable, private mechanism for practising personal skill and thinking ability. The following case description is an example from a self-coach in his own words.

SPOTTING BALONEY - MITCH'S SYSTEM

"I must own up to a tendency to believe. When I'm given information I usually take it at face value. A few times I've been caught out. So I've taught myself a little technique that I based on something I once read by Carl Sagan. He called it his baloney kit. I've adapted it to a quick and simple checklist and I train my personality (which is normally very unstructured) to use it. There are four parts to it. First, I list the facts and ask for confirmation. Second, when an idea is put forward, I always ask – 'What would the opposite be?" and open up a debate to check out other options, too. Third, I ask – "And what have you not told me about this?". And lastly, I ask for a list of the quantitative and the qualitative factors.

I've got to the point, where I can now rapidly work through some of this checklist in my head. It's taken time and I quite like working this way now, even though it has not come naturally to me".

If you possess the inclination, you can self-coach in all kinds of situations. Each example below requires a degree of personal discipline and a genuine desire to improve.

- Practise speaking at different paces to meet the needs of people with different communication styles and preferences.

- Take stock privately and purposefully of the ramifications of decisions you've made and what you might do differently another time.

- Put yourself in situations you do not find comfortable so as to stretch your own boundaries.

- When working as part of a team, put yourself, mentally, in the shoes of other team members to understand their thinking and to anticipate how you might influence them. (This technique can greatly speed up your influencing capacity).

- Practise adjusting and using language that would appeal to different styles.

- Work through data, practising speed of response to specific questions and finding your way more and more rapidly around the figures.

PAUSE FOR THOUGHT

The leadership calibres are about DOING.

Try auditing yourself:–

To what extent do you invest your own effort in: –

- Personally motivating others?

- Managing the performance of individuals in your care, including understanding why there are absences and errors?

- Preparing people for the future? – Change is a feature of business life everywhere. People who are flexible in meeting change contribute to a productive organisation

When you take stock of the way you lead people, do you sometimes find yourself excusing yourself on the grounds of your "day job"?

Galvanisers understand that people ARE their day job

GALVANISERS DEMONSTRATE NERVE
BY ASKING OTHERS TO AUDIT THEIR PERFORMANCE

CHAPTER FIVE

LOOK INTO THE MIRROR.
WHAT DO YOU SEE?
THE PERSON YOU ARE USED TO SEEING.
NOW, ASK OTHERS TO HOLD UP THAT MIRROR
AND DESCRIBE WHAT THEY SEE.
THEIR FRESH EYES
GIVE YOU FRESH EYES - AN INVALUABLE SAFETY NET
AND A TOOL FOR YOUR OWN PRODUCTIVITY.

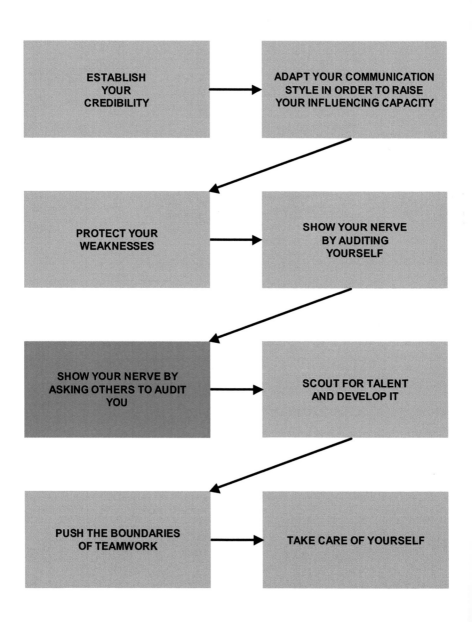

> **Chapter Five Snapshot**
>
> In addition to self-audit, galvanisers have the nerve to invite direct feedback from others in a systematic and structured way.
>
> This chapter describes a system of third-party audit called *Pairing for Performance*.
>
> Two participants comment on their own experience of this method.
>
> You are also offered two feedback frameworks which encourage methodical, evidence-based feedback.

Here's a rather radical way of making sure you stay in touch, especially if you happen to be a member of higher management. It's called *Pairing for Performance*.

It's a system of face-to-face, upward feedback which involves observation and feedback in real time and in real life situations. Here's how it works.

- Managers pair with volunteer members of staff (preferably from the front line). The emphasis on the front line is because they are the ones that ultimately deliver senior management promises. If front line staff are demotivated or confused, the whole organisation suffers.

- The purpose of this 'buddying' relationship is regular, constructive feedback on interpersonal performance. A *Pairing for Performance* relationship might last for months or years and one manager might have several buddies from different functions and levels.

- The pairs privately agree on the range of situations in which the manager would like direct feedback. These might be meetings, presentations, negotiations, regional visits or any situation through which the manager can learn how (s)he is viewed by front line staff. The focus of the pairing arrangement will vary from pair to pair, but a prime purpose for such a relationship is to keep senior managers in touch with how they and their messages are received at ground level.

- From time to time, the buddy observes the manager in live action and supplies structured, detailed feedback.

- An investment in developing the skills of buddies at the outset will repay you many times over. Buddies need to be skilled observers and communicators as well as relationship builders. The skill of feedback is vital to the success of the arrangement.

DAVE, ON BEING A BUDDY

"My initial feelings were about whether I had it in me to give feedback to someone who was five grades above me and far more experienced than myself. The confidence to give feedback has been my biggest stride. In the buddy workshops, we'd practised various feedback techniques before I tried them out for real. I've found – and this is what I'd say to anyone who, like me, finds the grade issue a problem – that, provided you pay attention and listen closely and use appropriate feedback techniques, you can give feedback to anyone in any situation, even with limited information.

"Helping others to see why people react to them in a particular way is rewarding. The biggest plus has been in seeing my paired manager operating differently – not in big ways but small adjustments which have made a difference to how he relates to his more junior members of staff. It's been noticeable by everyone in the team and I feel quite a lot of satisfaction that some of it anyway was down to my feedback.

"For me, it has been an enormous development opportunity. I've gained insights into how senior managers have to work, how they think and the range of demands on their time. I understand now the context in which they have to work. It has helped me to counteract some of my (at times) cynical views of higher management.

"The experience has also made me think about my own abilities and possibilities and it's added to my influencing ability. It's a new way of working for this organisation – and I like the feeling of being in at the start of something innovative.

" So it's been of benefit to me and to my paired manager. I would also add that there's got to be a benefit to the organisation because it is development in the workplace, rather than in the classroom and that must save on costs.

"The aspects that have tested me have been:-

- o making the time to observe and give feedback regularly enough for it to be meaningful (otherwise you don't pick up patterns of behaviour),

- o concentrating on details in my observation in order to be able to supply good information (like the language my paired manager uses to get his message across and when and where it is most or least successful),

- o managing the relationship – I have to remember that I am, in effect, a service supplier to my paired manager. The main purpose in the buddying arrangement is his development, not mine. Sometimes, this means responding to a request to be present at an event when it might not be wholly convenient.

"I think that organisations miss something in not using this kind of system more often. Developing working relationships that can work successfully across grade boundaries has got to be good for communication, understanding and efficiency in any organisation."

ON BEING BUDDIED

Jayne's tips on the attitudes needed by the buddied

"Buddying breaks the mould of hierarchical mindsets and traditions. The first attitude that is needed is to see people as they are, not as a 'position'. In a hierarchical culture, people are often labelled – "secretary", "receptionist", "management potential", "no management potential". Labels can write off people for years to come. Labels psychologically discourage us from moving on our attitudes about each other. This may be why so many people have to leave organisations to advance – going to new environments where they have not (yet) been labelled.

"Imagine you are Sandra. She was my buddy in the Vanilla Pairing for Performance system. She helped me to transform my relationship with my manager, a relationship with which I had been struggling for months. Her fresh eyes observed what I had failed to observe about the mismatch in our communication methods. Her straightforward feedback and suggestions persuaded me to adjust my style of communication – to have facts and detail at hand, to be structured, not go-with-the-flow, in my style.

"When I say transform I mean that I now no longer struggle to influence my manager. What took hours and several attempts to get agreement on in the past, now takes minutes. A productivity gain for sure - add up the senior management time spent on meetings that produce no outcomes or, worse still, are counter-productive.

"Before Sandra worked as my buddy I probably did not give her much thought at all, except to see her as a secretary who had been around for some time. But I've got to know her well. And this is her story. I tell it because we are all too good, we senior managers, at dismissing the Sandras of this world, or not seeing them as being as valuable as the external consultants whose advice and guidance we so often purchase.

"Sandra's tale, then:-

"Sandra has worked as a secretary for the same manager and his team, in the same organisation for over seven years. She has risen to a position of trust and confidentiality because she has demonstrated utter reliability, considerable initiative, an unerring sense of responsibility in her work, and immense adaptability in absorbing, without fuss, ever changing duties, technology, processes and personal demands from the frenetically-paced team she serves.

"Having recognised the need to bring service standards to a high level, she has quietly lobbied every senior manager and obtained support for a service improvement group involving first the senior secretaries and then all the administrative staff (some 120 of them) in the organisation. Together they have examined the blocks to communication, they have streamlined some of their processes, they have started a bi-weekly lunch-time development group to which they invite internal and external speakers in order to improve their business understanding and to add to their skills.

"Newcomers are brought into this lunch-time exercise from the start of their employment. They invite their own managers to some of these sessions in order to keep them involved and aware.

"Over the months there is a buzz about the place and higher and higher expectations of what the administrative team will deliver. Sandra and her co-workers have worked hard to influence a range of attitudes, from the reluctant and uncertain, to the cynical and dismissive.

"Sandra and her team mates have demonstrated some first class change consultancy skills right under the noses of their most senior managers.

"But when our organisation merged with another, we brought in a reputable consultancy firm to help us scope and implement a change programme. Because, you see, the mindset of the senior management team (us) was in such a rut that no internal person was considered worth releasing for this important step in organisational growth, or to possess what it takes to undertake such a responsibility.

"And certainly no one labelled 'a secretary', despite the hard evidence to the contrary, could possibly be considered a 'credible' consultant.

"What is more, Sandra has limited her own mindset about herself and her capability beyond the role of secretary. She seems shy of her own capacity for revolutionising working practice".

Jayne's description of Sandra is not so unusual. Sandra is not alone. I have found many Sandras in organisations among supervisors, managers, trainers, engineers, shop stewards, customer service co-ordinators, personnel administrators, and the list goes on. They have all, in their individual ways, contributed to the improvement of their own working arrangements, and, therefore, to their organisation.

But neither they, nor their organisations, have seriously thought of the possibilities for transferring their ingenuity beyond their immediate job boundaries. Or, if they have, perhaps it has been viewed as far too much trouble to orchestrate in any really radical way in order to transform, rather than tinker with, working practice.

They are all part of a culture that invests in training and development, and the so-called cross-fertilisation of knowledge, but hesitates from calling upon that considerable and important investment when it is most needed. Yet, with a degree of leadership, organisation and support, a wealth of promise could be unleashed to transform a working operation.

Galvanisers are true *change leaders*. A galvaniser will challenge these mindsets and break the mould, seeing people as they really are.

> *"...people may have met twenty times before seeing one another. 'Seeing' has an active side and a passive one. Most people we run across mean so little to us that we never bestir ourselves to look at them..."*
> W. Somerset Maugham, The Book Bag.

Meaningful, well-delivered feedback is critical to the success of the Pairing for Performance system. For feedback to be really valuable, it needs to be precise, relevant and supported by evidence and pin-pointed examples. Dave's view in the first of the preceding case studies shows how anxious people can become when they are providing feedback.

It has been a surprise to me to hear some people in organisations describe the giving and receiving of feedback as a "pink and fluffy" activity. The term 'pink and fluffy' implies soft and easy. Yet, giving honest feedback is anything but easy. This may explain why so many organisations opt for 360 ° feedback where the receiver does not know whose comments (s)he is receiving because they are anonymously presented. In fact, face-to-face feedback takes skill and guts. It also takes practice and it is helped by using an easily-applied framework.

You can encourage thorough, evidence-based feedback by applying an at-a-glance system such as the SEEDS feedback framework or the NERVE-JUDGEMENT feedback framework in the following pages. Both encourage the giver of feedback to focus on specifics.

THE SEEDS FEEDBACK FRAMEWORK

Feedback becomes easier to receive if the giver of feedback is clear and precise.

S PECIFY THE CONTEXT

Set the context clearly. Start by reminding the receiver of feedback of the exact situation to which the feedback refers – e.g. date, time, circumstance – anything that will help the other person to recall.

E PISODE

Describe the episode in as much detail as possible – e.g. the behaviour observed, statements made, specific words used.

E FFECT

Describe the *positive* impact of the behaviour.

D OWNSIDE (if appropriate)

Describe the *negative* impact of the behaviour.

S UGGESTION for improvement of the downside.

THE NERVE-JUDGEMENT FRAMEWORK

The receiver of feedback may also wish to identify specific categories of behaviour that are to be the subject of observation and feedback.

The *Nerve-Judgement Observation Framework** below is one such example in which management behaviour that shows nerve and demonstrates judgement are used as the basis for very specific observations.

NERVE

COURAGE

Example - the readiness to take a risk or to stand out from the crowd in order to move people or an organisation on.

NO EXCUSES

Example - Tackling difficult situations and people, taking ownership of performance issues.

STAMINA

Example – Showing resilience in the face of hostility and tenacity in the face of continuing organisational change.

* **shortened** *version of the Nerve-Judgement Framework from Vanilla Room to Master®*

JUDGEMENT

STREET CRED

Example - Judging how to use language to translate corporate mission into a meaningful format for others, and then acting on that judgement.

TRANSFER OF EXPERTISE

Example – Judging when, how and to whom to transfer personal knowledge and expertise.

BLEND OF TOUGHNESS & SENSITIVITY

Example – Judging when and how to vary communication and influencing style.

PAUSE FOR THOUGHT

How often do you seek feedback on your personal performance *outside* 'official' processes such as appraisals?

When was the last time you acted on feedback on your behaviour? What was the result?

GALVANISERS SCOUT FOR
AND DEVELOP FUTURE TALENT
IN ORDER TO SAFEGUARD
THE BUSINESS

CHAPTER SIX

NO ORGANISATION CAN SURVIVE WITHOUT
SCOUTING FOR TALENT TO
REPLENISH,
REINVIGORATE,
RESTORE
ITS CAPABILITY.
SO, IF YOU ARE PART OF AN ORGANISATION,
IT IS IN YOUR OWN INTERESTS
TO DEVELOP OTHERS.

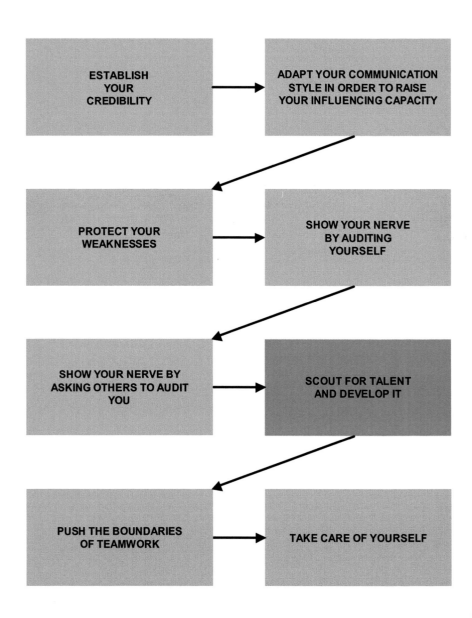

Scouting for talent is a critical part of the galvaniser's method. The future of the organisation depends on a flow of capable, well prepared workers in every function and at every level, including successors to senior management.

Galvanisers will always keep an eye on succession in their own areas, involving themselves personally where necessary in the process of coaching – identifying, preparing, energising and releasing their future talent.

In the workplace, coaching opportunities abound and galvanisers understand the value of this kind of interpersonal connection both to the coach and to the learner – two-way support, two-way learning, two-way understanding and two-way energising.

Effective coaching needs a system as well as skills. The *PLUS 3* system of coaching assists the galvaniser to choose an appropriate response to the learner. Emphasising the significance of lining up the coach' s style with the learner, the *PLUS 3* system will help the coach:-

- To choose the best communication style,

- To identify the right level of coaching,

- To align the coaching relationship.

THREE ELEMENTS OF THE *PLUS 3* SYSTEM

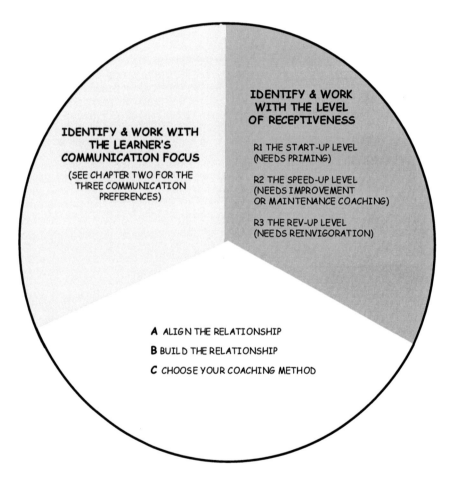

IDENTIFY & WORK WITH THE LEARNER'S COMMUNICATION FOCUS

(SEE CHAPTER TWO FOR THE THREE COMMUNICATION PREFERENCES)

IDENTIFY & WORK WITH THE LEVEL OF RECEPTIVENESS

R1 THE START-UP LEVEL (NEEDS PRIMING)

R2 THE SPEED-UP LEVEL (NEEDS IMPROVEMENT OR MAINTENANCE COACHING)

R3 THE REV-UP LEVEL (NEEDS REINVIGORATION)

A ALIGN THE RELATIONSHIP

B BUILD THE RELATIONSHIP

C CHOOSE YOUR COACHING METHOD

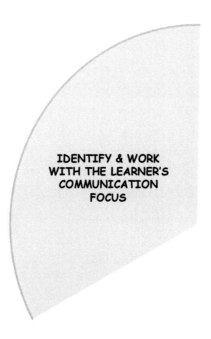

**IDENTIFY & WORK
WITH THE LEARNER'S
COMMUNICATION
FOCUS**

Thoughtful coaching starts with the other person, not with the coach. If you want to assist people on the road to a new level of performance, you first have to meet them where they are.

Choose the right mode of communication – refresh your memory about the three communication preferences in Chapter Two and adjust your style accordingly.

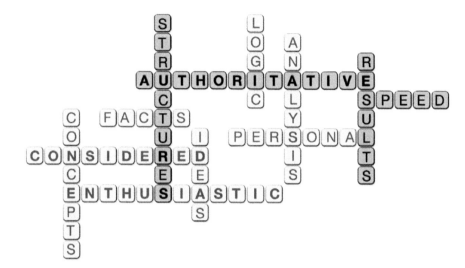

So, if you are coaching someone operating in the 'authoritative' mode, you would use short sentences and plain language, you would back up your suggestions with evidence and you would adopt an organised approach.

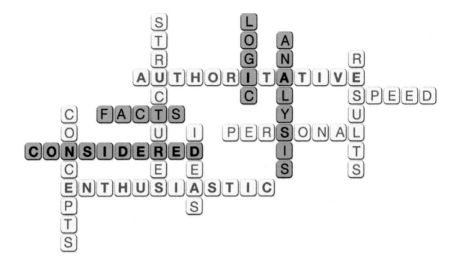

If you are coaching someone operating in the 'considered' mode, you would give plenty of time and space for reflection, you would use a moderate pace, you would have to hand your facts and data, you would speak in practical rather than conceptual terms.

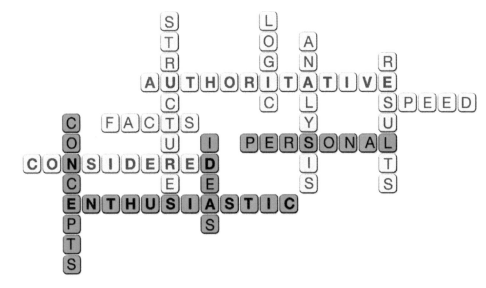

If you are coaching someone operating in the 'enthusiastic' mode, you would allow room for digression and anecdote, you would use a light structure, you would offer a wide range of sometimes experimental options.

It is important to adjust your communication style because people relate best to those who are like them and lining up your communication style with the person you are trying to coach makes for a productive working relationship.

**IDENTIFY & WORK
WITH THE LEVEL
OF RECEPTIVENESS**

R1 THE START-UP LEVEL
(NEEDS PRIMING)

R2 THE SPEED-UP LEVEL
(NEEDS IMPROVEMENT
OR MAINTENANCE COACHING)

R3 THE REV-UP LEVEL
(NEEDS REINVIGORATION)

Element Two of the Plus 3 system requires the coach to understand the other person's level of receptiveness so that coaching effort and time is not wasted and is matched to the need.

R1 – The 'Start-Up' Level

A person operating at this level might be new into the job or organisation and in need of **initial** coaching in standards and expectations.

R2 – The 'Speed-Up' Level

A person operating at this level might want to progress further in the organisation and may be in need of some advanced techniques and knowledge.

R3 – The 'Rev-Up' Level

A person operating at this level might be reaching the end of a career or working in a long held job and may be in need of reinvigoration, such as leading a special project to capitalise on experience and organisational knowledge.

A ALIGN THE RELATIONSHIP

B BUILD THE RELATIONSHIP

C CHOOSE YOUR COACHING METHOD

Phasing a coaching relationship

There is a logical sequence in developing a coaching relationship, especially a new coaching relationship – the ABC sequence: -

A lign your style with the style and need of the client.

B uild your understanding of each other.

C hoose your coaching approach – the skills you use in the course of a coaching relationship may range from the reflective to the prescriptive depending on the situation and the client (see the Attending, Building and Controlling skills on the following pages).

A RANGE OF CONVERSATIONAL SKILLS APPLIED TO COACHING

Coaching, like any form of influencing, draws on the systematic use of conversational devices – attending skills, building skills, and controlling skills.

ATTENDING SKILLS

Proximity
Judge the space you need to give the other person.

Eye Contact
You should be able to make easy eye contact.

Continuation Prompts
These are signs of encouragement – for example, non-verbal signs (nods, smiles) or verbal encouragement ("Good point", "Aha/Mm", or repeating the speaker's final words (known as *final word acknowledgements*).

Reflective Listening
Reflecting back the gist of what you have heard to demonstrate your attention, interest and understanding.

BUILDING SKILLS

Clarifying

"So, if I understood you.."

"May I just clarify..?"

Linking

"That's very similar to the suggestion we made earlier..."

"I'd like to pick up on an earlier point..."

Expanding

"May we add something to that...?"

"Yes..and we could also look at it as..."

Seeking agreement

"Are we all agreed, then...?"

"To what extent are we able to agree on...?"

Proposing

"Let's consider..."

"What about an alternative course of action, such as..?"

Summarising

Summarising is both a control mechanism and a way of clarifying

Non-verbal cues

Gestures to invite a contribution, or to control or interrupt the flow of discussion

Guiding

"Could we stop there, just for a moment, in order to..."

Probing

"Could I ask you to take me through your reasoning here?"

Flagging/Signposting

"Let's now move on to the second point"

Questions

Open and closed questions to develop the discussion.

Open questions encourage expansion – e.g. "To what extent does this match your view of things?"

Closed questions help to contain or limit contributions – e.g. "Is this correct?"

PAUSE FOR THOUGHT

Securing the future of a business is partly about strategy and very much about having a stream of people who can fulfil that strategy.

It is easy to offload this responsibility to trainers when it is, in fact, a prime duty for anyone with responsibility for people at any level. (Remind yourself of the leadership calibres in Chapter Four).

When was the last time you took a personal hand in developing others?

What was the result?

What did you learn from it?

Where were you most effective?

What could you do about the areas where you were less effective?

GALVANISERS PUSH THE BOUNDARIES
OF TEAMWORK

CHAPTER SEVEN

TEAMS NEED CONSTANT REINVIGORATION
AND CHALLENGING OR THEY WILL GROW STALE,
TOO ACCUSTOMED TO EACH OTHER TO BE HONEST,
TOO PROTECTIVE TO DARE,
TOO INSULAR TO EXPERIMENT.
INVIGORATED TEAMWORK IS CRUCIAL
TO ORGANISATIONAL SUCCESS.

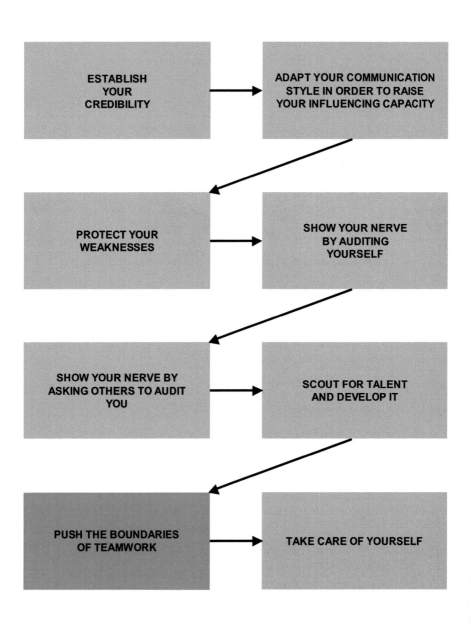

ESTABLISH YOUR CREDIBILITY → ADAPT YOUR COMMUNICATION STYLE IN ORDER TO RAISE YOUR INFLUENCING CAPACITY

PROTECT YOUR WEAKNESSES → SHOW YOUR NERVE BY AUDITING YOURSELF

SHOW YOUR NERVE BY ASKING OTHERS TO AUDIT YOU → SCOUT FOR TALENT AND DEVELOP IT

PUSH THE BOUNDARIES OF TEAMWORK → TAKE CARE OF YOURSELF

THE BALANCING ACT

The best teams are balanced. They cover for each other. They learn from each other and about each other. They challenge each other. They keep on the move. One of the great features of really effective teams is the standards of behaviour they set for themselves *at the outset*.

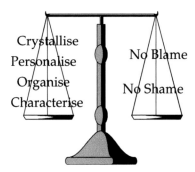

Try *The Balancing Act* in your own team. On the left hand side of the scale are the behaviours you commit to doing. On the right hand side of the scale are the behaviours you commit to avoiding.

1.   Crystallise

First in the balance is the way you express your vision, goals and standards of conduct as a team. (Example – "We will work with our suppliers as one team").

2.   Personalise

Second in the balance is the way you apply those standards to each individual member of the team, including how you will support and coach each other and tackle difficult issues within the team. (Some examples of the areas team standards might cover – communication, speed of response, timely briefings, format of reports, timely feedback to prevent misunderstandings).

3.   Organise

Third in the balance is how you will organise yourselves for effectiveness. This is about the wise and honest use of your skills and experience. (See Chapter Three on the Prime Mover and the Dedicated Ambassadors for some tips).

4.   Characterise

Characterising is about being role models. So, fourth in the balance is the way the team will ensure others can see and learn from their strengths and organisation, as well as from their mistakes – demonstrating openly that they live up to high standards so that others will want to join or emulate the team.

5.   No Blame

On the other side of the balance is the avoidance of negative behaviour. 'No Blame' does not mean 'No Accountability'. In behavioural terms it means a shift from recrimination and finger-pointing to resolving mistakes and understanding their root cause so that they can be avoided the next time.   Blaming is time-wasting and alienating. Understanding and learning are fruitful and motivating.

6.   No Shame

This is linked to No Blame. If team members are confident that they will not be made scapegoats, they are more likely to acknowledge errors and learn from them. It's important to reflect that No Blame and No Shame behaviours are not timid. They are the disciplined actions of people of grit and steely determination.

HONESTY - IN - ACTION SESSIONS

Galvanisers will also find ways to keep their teams on their toes, while retaining the comfort of a family relationship. *Honesty-in-Action Sessions* (HIAS) such as the one described below develop a daring honesty. They require non-rivalrous attitudes and a courageous, 'up for it' mentality.

BARRY'S HONESTY - IN - ACTION SESSION

Barry is the head of a department. His organisation has recently invested in a change programme to move its style away from centralised and hierarchical decision-making, which focused the responsibilty for decisions on a few, to one of encouraging decision-making at all levels. He has five managers directly reporting to him who have been used to Barry's fairly tight rein on decisions within the team. All the managers have a date every month in their diaries for a three-hour joint session with Barry. Their purpose is to recognise good practice, to tackle potential problems early, to air issues, to prevent what Barry calls 'corridor griping', and to learn from mistakes. The sessions typically begin like this:-

Barry
"Today I think it is Gill's turn to kick off. What would you like to highlight, Gill?"

*Gill goes through points about various members of the team, including Barry, to identify **her own perception and experience** of her association with each of them over the preceding month. To help her do this, she refers back to her own 'Recollections Jotting Book' which refreshes her memory. She is not permitted to make statements without evidence (hence the notebook). Here is an example of her comments, which cover both compliments and criticism.*

Gill
"First of all, I'd like to thank Jenny for her support earlier this month. I was dealing with a complex disciplinary issue. I don't think it's appropriate to go into details, but I would like to say that the time and the listening ear that Jenny offered made a great deal of difference to how I felt about tackling it.

"The second point I would like to make is about a particular incident that highlights the way in which we can, without thinking, undermine each other. One of my staff – Jane Smith – bypassed me to go to Barry (incidentally, Barry knows I'd intended to raise this point because I had already discussed it with him). Without realising it, Barry made a decision which overruled what I'd agreed with Jane. I realise there are times when we are all under pressure, but it's the kind of thing that breaks trust. All it required was for you, Barry, to hold off until you had spoken to me. However, you were honest enough to own up to the mistake, and I suppose it is a feature of the newness of the consultative style we have chosen to adopt in place of our old style of referring all decisions to Barry. The difficult issue for the two of us now is how we deal with Jane, who has conflicting responses from two managers, and, presumably, sees me as being easy to override if she puts her case convincingly enough to Barry. We thought it would be a valuable issue for us to discuss as a team – as a way of examining our own consistency and perhaps agreeing a process for this and other potential areas of confusion."

[Group discussion followed before Gill continued with her next point].

Each member of the team is invited to make her/his comments. There is no requirement to say something about everyone. Each person sets his or her own agenda. Sometimes, if an issue is important enough, the team agrees to dedicate extra time to it on a separate occasion.

The significant feature of this kind of galvanising behaviour is that it extends teamwork beyond the norm. It requires attention to details (such as the system to which the team will work - system and ground rules act as a safety net). It aims for a high degree of open behaviour which then enables the team to nip potential conflict in the bud where otherwise it would end up consuming valuable time and depleting team productivity.

4x = HPT – A MODEL FOR HIGH PERFORMING TEAMS

Galvanisers push the boundaries of what it is to work as a team. In the following model for developing High Performing Teams, the Honesty-in-Action session, such as the one described above, might form part of the 'Exchange' stream where 'openly delivered feedback' is one of the criteria for advanced team conduct.

The model is in two sections.

The first part of the model supplies four streams which are continuously worked in order to develop high team performance.

The second part of the model draws attention to specific areas that the team leader needs to deliver to the team.

A MODEL FOR HIGH PERFORMING TEAMS

4x = HPT

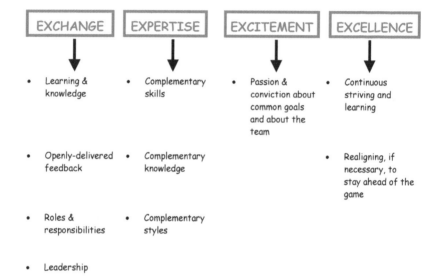

EXCHANGE	EXPERTISE	EXCITEMENT	EXCELLENCE
• Learning & knowledge	• Complementary skills	• Passion & conviction about common goals and about the team	• Continuous striving and learning
• Openly-delivered feedback	• Complementary knowledge		• Realigning, if necessary, to stay ahead of the game
• Roles & responsibilities	• Complementary styles		
• Leadership			

Leadership Implications = C x 5

- *Co-creating common goals & values*

- *Communicating excitement & belief*

- *Capitalising on the skills, knowledge, & styles within the team in order to align to goals*

- *Correcting misalignment*

- *Contributing personal commitment, energy, & support*

PART ONE OF THE MODEL (4X= HPT) - The galvaniser continuously works these four streams in order to develop high team performance:-

- o **Exchange** – sharing knowledge, views and responsibilities. High performing teams will even share the leadership of the team, using a different person as leader for different situations.
- o **Expertise** – ensuring there are complementary styles and skills in the team.
- o **Excitement** – generating enthusiasm for the work of the team and for being part of the team.
- o **Excellence** – striving for continuous improvement in the operation and behaviour of the team.

PART TWO OF THE MODEL (C x 5) – Five aspects of the team leader's ***behaviour*** make a special contribution to team performance:-

- o Ensuring buy-in to team goals by co-creating them (i.e. the team is not 'told' them but develops them together).
- o Inspiring a strong belief in themselves - as individuals and as a collective force.
- o Making the most of the skills and knowledge in the team at all times, constantly revisiting and updating these.
- o Ensuring standards are consistent across the team – checking, aligning and realigning team conduct and team standards.
- o Demonstrating a strong personal commitment to the team, its goals and standards (acting as a role model).

PAUSE FOR THOUGHT

Without workable teams, we do not have workable organisations. Successful teamwork is almost entirely about how the team members behave towards each other.

In what ways do you invest in advanced team behaviour?

What has worked most easily?

What has produced the best results?

Which are the areas of teamwork that you find yourself constantly addressing? For what reasons?

Which are the very best teams of your experience? What differentiates them from other teams? (Look back over the models for high performing teams – you may find that these ingredients were present in your best teams).

What do you do/can you do to transfer the experience of your best teams to others?

GALVANISERS TAKE CARE
OF THEMSELVES

CHAPTER EIGHT

GALVANISERS INVEST IN THEMSELVES.
IT IS TOO EASY TO BE DRIVEN ALONG BY THE PACE OF LIFE
ALWAYS SAYING "TOMORROW,"
BUT THERE'S A SAYING
'IF WE DON'T KNOW WHERE WE ARE HEADED,
WE'LL END UP SOME PLACE ELSE.'
IF WE DON'T WANT REGRETS, IT MAKES GOOD SENSE
TO TAKE TIME-OUTS NOW AND THEN,
TO TAKE A GOOD HONEST LOOK AT OURSELVES
AND RECALIBRATE IF NECESSARY.

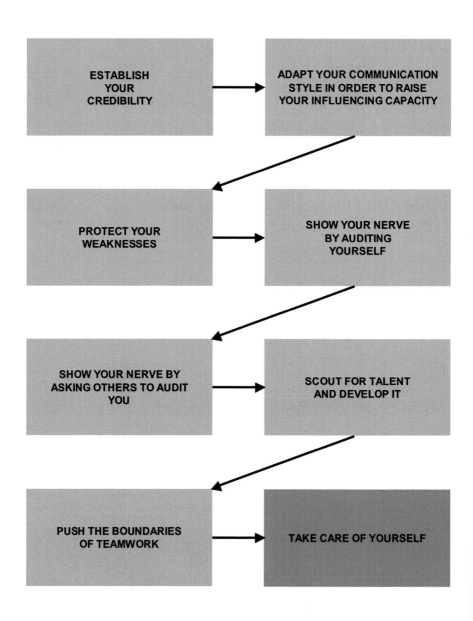

Chapter Eight Snapshot

Galvanisers refresh their own plans and strategies, review their motives and check on their personal aspirations. They do this in order to recharge their energy and motivation and because taking care of oneself is a sensible business and personal strategy.

This chapter introduces you to three caretaking frameworks – two systems for personal stocktaking and a technique for identifying allies to help you to safeguard your goals.

Even the most robust machine needs maintenance and an overhaul now and then. Galvanisers understand this for themselves, as well as for their people. Sometimes they will organise team away-days. Sometimes they will encourage career-planning events. Sometimes, they take time-outs *for themselves*, to look back and take stock, to look ahead and prepare, and to check that they are still happy to be where they are and, if not, to do something about it.

This is the last, but essential, element of a galvaniser's system – personal caretaking.

Personal caretaking is the process of self-awareness and self-development which requires all the Vanilla elements:-

- innovation (Vulcan),

- good sense (Athena),

- seeking feedback on how others see you (Nereus),

- a degree of courage and risk taking (Icarus),

- a desire to raise your own game (Ludus),

- aiming for higher and higher standards (Laureus)

and

- clarity of purpose (Apollo).

Here are three caretaking frameworks.

Framework One – A structure of stocktaking questions to ask yourself.

Framework Two – Safeguarding your goals through the calibre of your front line – the people who deliver for you.

Framework Three - A table of 'Vanilla' indicators called The Seven Mirrors. You can use it to test your own track record as a galvaniser or as a set of the behaviours you could deploy to add to your reputation as a galvaniser of people.

Framework One – Three Perspectives

There are a number of aspects you could consider under the Three Perspectives.

1. **LOOK BACK**

2. **LOOK AROUND**

3. **LOOK AHEAD**

1. LOOK BACK

- Take the last six months.

- Devise a bar chart showing the highs and lows.

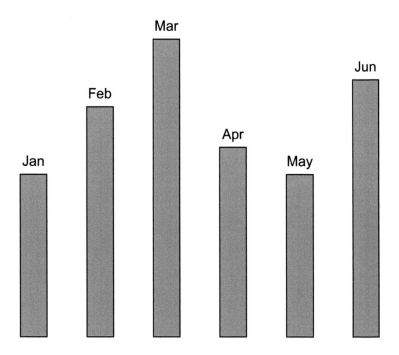

- Make a record of the particular points and memories that are especially significant to you in this period by annotating the chart or writing a separate narrative.

- Analyse –

    (i)   What happened and what did I do to make it happen?

    (ii)   How exactly did I make it happen (e.g. skills used, people used)?

    (iii)   What did I learn for another time?

    (iv)   Have I applied that learning? If so, how and what was the result?

2.   LOOK AROUND

Am I happy with the current situation? You may wish to consider some of these (but don't be constrained by them):-

- Intangible achievements (e.g. reputation, personal image, self esteem)

- Tangible achievements (e.g. business results, performance data)

- Working relationships

- Sense of the organisational community

- Sense of purpose

- Personal Impact – e.g. impact on your health, status, security

3. LOOK AHEAD

- How much of (2) above do I still want to reach?

- Will my current position enable me to reach them?

- If not, what changes do I need to and want to make, and in what timescale?

- If yes, what adjustments, if any, do I need to make?

- Will anything but myself stop me?

- If so, WHAT?

- How MUCH of a barrier is it?

- How can I get over the barrier and in what timescale?

Framework Two – The Front Line

Caretaking is also about gathering around you a network of allies who can spread your standards and expectations. In their search for continuous improvement, galvanisers need the very best in their front line. This is as much about attitude as skill.

Here's an approach, called *Rich Thinking and Restricted Thinking*, which a galvaniser can use as a set of clues to spot and enlist those front line supporters.

Galvanisers will use the rich thinkers as their natural allies. They look for rich thinkers at every level, overleaping hierarchical boundaries if necessary,

They will also find ways, through coaching, to utilise the restricted thinkers. For example, restricted thinkers can serve as a useful feasibility-check, pointing out the pitfalls that others may, in their enthusiasm, overlook.

RICH THINKERS

RESTRICTED THINKERS

TALK OF INVESTMENTS, BENEFITS, VALUE

TALK OF COSTS

HAVE THEIR EYE ON THE PRIZE AT THE END (E.G. THE GOAL OF THE PROJECT / THEIR OWN CAREER GOALS)

SEE MAINLY THE CONTSTRAINTS & BOUNDARIES OF THE IMMEDIATE MOMENT

TEND TO ASK 'HOW?'

TEND TO ASK 'WHY?'

VIVIDLY SEE THE POSSIBILITIES & POTENTIAL (OFFER IDEAS)

FEAR FOR THE PENALTIES & REPRIMANDS (OFFER EXCUSES)

LOOK AROUND & THINK AHEAD (SEEK ACTIVE INVOLVEMENT)

LOOK DOWN & AWAY (RECOIL FROM INVOLVEMENT)

ADOPT THE RESOLVER'S PHILOSOPHY - 'LOOK & YOU MAY NOT SEE, THINK AND YOU MAY NOT SEE, BUT THE TWO TOGETHER WILL RESOLVE THE ISSUE'

ADOPT THE RELEGATOR'S PHILOSOPHY - 'LOOK TO ANOTHER'

So, you've spotted your network of potential allies. Winning them means being gutsy and honest about what you are about. It is alright to say "We are about to start doing what isn't the done thing around here" often enough until it becomes the done thing. That's what galvanising is about. Facing the discomfort.

Think of your network of allies like an intricate timepiece. The delicate mechanism, however carefully assembled, may become loose and disengage. Setting up your network is only the beginning. Care, alertness and recuperation will keep it in good working order.

Sometimes parts of it will need to be replaced. Get everyone ready for this – it is part of the honesty of the galvaniser's approach.

Some timepieces will work amidst the risks and efforts of the deep sea diver. Others will be the dress model. Others will be the workaday variety. Your allies can be deployed in the circumstances that best suit them to make the most of their particular qualities and inclination. Galvanisers give quality help to those who are really serious about doing things differently.

Framework Three – Vanilla Indicators – The Seven Mirrors

Galvanisers work at a range of different levels and with different methods to maintain their connection with people.

Personal caretaking includes vetting your own methodology as a galvaniser. You could use the set of indicators on the following pages as a measure of your own range and as a barometer of when and how you tend to work the different qualities of the Galvaniser (e.g. when are you working the Vulcan side, or Athena etc?).

Against each of the Vanilla elements are examples of the areas which you might work into your modus operandi as a galvaniser. For convenient reference, the elements are also supplied in table form.

You are working your VULCAN side when you are
gutsy and innovative

Working On Yourself	Developing the capacity to think of yourself and your situation differently
Developing The Potential You See In Others	Developing innovative ways to manage people
Raising Your Own Leadership Standards	Developing your capacity for creative problem-solving
Pushing The Boundaries Of Teamwork	Developing your team's innovation and creativity

You are working your ATHENA side when you are demonstrating your understanding, awareness, and good sense

Working On Yourself	Developing an understanding, appreciation and awareness of your own possibilities
Developing The Potential You See In Others	Capitalising on the wisdom and knowledge of others
Raising Your Own Leadership Standards	Developing your understanding and skill in reaching and influencing others
Pushing The Boundaries Of Teamwork	Developing a team's capacity to capitalise on each others' strengths

You are working your NEREUS side when you seek feedback and demonstrate the capacity to put yourself into the shoes of another

Working On Yourself	Appreciating the impact you and your decisions have on others
Developing The Potential You See In Others	Developing the capacity to tune into different communication styles and needs
Raising Your Own Leadership Standards	Developing your appreciation of how you are seen by the people you seek to lead and inspire
Pushing The Boundaries Of Teamwork	Developing a team's feedback skills

You are working your ICARUS side when you demonstrate your judgement in taking a risk

Working On Yourself	Developing the nerve to take yourself out of your comfort zone
Developing The Potential You See In Others	Developing the skills to challenge and confront effectively
Raising Your Own Leadership Standards	Breaking the mould in who you gather around you to improve your capability
Pushing The Boundaries Of Teamwork	Developing a team's capacity for well-considered risk taking

You are working your LUDUS side when you lay out a clear
game-plan for yourself and others

Working On Yourself	Developing clarity about your general and specific aspirations - stocktaking and recalibrating
Developing The Potential You See In Others	Developing clear structures and frameworks for succession planning
Raising Your Own Leadership Standards	Raising your own standards (and helping to raise the standards of others) in visioning, goal planning and contingency planning
Pushing The Boundaries Of Teamwork	Raising a team's capacity for forward planning

You are working your LAUREUS side when you set, revisit, review and continuously emphasise high standards, taking tough decisions on managing performance if necessary

Working On Yourself	Setting unequivocal standards for your own behaviour
Developing The Potential You See In Others	Developing a system to ensure others work to high behavioural standards
Raising Your Own Leadership Standards	Personally coaching others to meet high behavioural standards
Pushing The Boundaries Of Teamwork	Working with teams on raising their behavioural standards

You are working your APOLLO side when you are helping others to make sense of goals, objectives or organisational complexity

Working On Yourself	Working with and balancing the tensions and conflicting needs in your own life
Developing The Potential You See In Others	Helping others to work with organisational goals. Simplifying the language of organisational missions if necessary
Raising Your Own Leadership Standards	Coaching your key people as your representatives in transmitting your long-term vision
Pushing The Boundaries Of Teamwork	Working together to create a vision for the team

A SUMMARY OF THE INDICATORS

LOOK INTO THE SEVEN MIRRORS	WORKING ON YOURSELF	DEVELOPING THE POTENTIAL YOU SEE IN OTHERS	RAISING YOUR OWN LEADERSHIP STANDARDS	PUSHING THE BOUNDARIES OF TEAMWORK
You are working your VULCAN side when you are gutsy and innovative	Developing the capacity to think of yourself and your situation differently	Developing innovative ways to manage people	Developing your capacity for creative problem-solving	Developing your team's innovation and creativity
You are working your ATHENA side when you are demonstrating your understanding, awareness, and good sense	Developing an understanding, appreciation and awareness of your own possibilities	Capitalising on the wisdom and knowledge of others	Developing your understanding and skill in reaching and influencing others	Developing a team's capacity to capitalise on each others' strengths
You are working your NEREUS side when you seek feedback and demonstrate the capacity to put yourself into the shoes of another	Appreciating the impact you and your decisions have on others	Developing the capacity to tune into different communication styles and needs	Developing your appreciation of how you are seen by the people you seek to lead and inspire	Developing a team's feedback skills
You are working your ICARUS side when you demonstrate your judgement in taking a risk	Developing the nerve to take yourself out of your comfort zone	Developing the skills to challenge and confront effectively	Breaking the mould in who you gather around you to improve your capability	Developing a team's capacity for well considered risk taking

A SUMMARY OF THE INDICATORS (continued)

LOOK INTO THE SEVEN MIRRORS	WORKING ON YOURSELF	DEVELOPING THE POTENTIAL YOU SEE IN OTHERS	RAISING YOUR OWN LEADERSHIP STANDARDS	PUSHING THE BOUNDARIES OF TEAMWORK
You are working your LUDUS side when you lay out a clear game-plan for yourself and others	Developing clarity about your general and specific aspirations – stocktaking and recalibrating	Developing clear structures and frameworks for succession planning	Raising your own standards (and helping to raise the standards of others) in visioning, goal planning and contingency planning	Raising a team's capacity for forward planning
You are working your LAUREUS side when you set, revisit, review and continuously emphasise high standards, taking tough decisions on managing performance if necessary	Setting unequivocal standards for your own behaviour	Developing a system to ensure others work to high behavioural standards	Personally coaching others to meet high behavioural standards	Working with teams on raising their behavioural standards
You are working your APOLLO side when you are helping others to make sense of goals, objectives or organisational complexity	Working with and balancing the tensions and conflicting needs in your own life	Helping others to work with organisational goals Simplifying the language of organisational missions if necessary	Coaching your key people as your representatives in transmitting your long-term vision	Working together to create a vision for the team

PAUSE FOR THOUGHT

How often do you give yourself real time and space? This question is about genuine time FOR YOU, rather than time spent with the family, or with friends, or with others who may need you.

When was the last time you methodically analysed where you are heading and why?

Looking after yourself is an essential galvanising ingredient. When others need you, it makes sense to fortify yourself at regular intervals.

A FINAL PAUSE FOR THOUGHT

Organisations need galvanisers because they are the ones who motivate others to higher and higher levels of performance. The skills they use are everyday human skills. In this sense they are not much different from the rest of us. It is the *application* of their human skills that makes them stand out - they apply their interpersonal ability with rigour, purpose and system.

The sense of privilege that I feel in having been able to see their qualities in action is tempered a little by the chastening thought that so much capability lies unused in organisations. Terms like 'soft skills' and 'hard skills' are commonly used in business these days to differentiate between interpersonal skills and operational know-how. Perhaps they only serve to erect a false division between the elements that deliver business success in any organisation.

People who are motivated, whose performance is well managed and who are developed and made ready for the future WILL deliver and KEEP delivering. What's more they make life easy for their leaders who can trust them to get on with things.

Galvanisers know this. That's why they invest in the quality of their contact with their people - those 'soft skills'. They do it without apology because it is soft skills, not structure, processes and procedures, that persuade, encourage, fire up and mobilise.

They are, in fact, the very essence of business performance.

THE VANILLA CONCEPT

 VULCAN - courage and innovation

 ATHENA - grounded common sense

 NEREUS - the capacity to put oneself in the shoes of another

 ICARUS – the readiness to take a risk

 LUDUS – continuous development of the game plan

 LAUREUS – continuous investment in high standards

 APOLLO - Casting light and clarity on complexity

SUMMARY OF TERMS, TOOLS & TECHNIQUES

THE REFERENCE AND SOURCE	CHAPTER
TL² – a role model's model (from Room To Master)	Chapter 1
A COMMUNICATOR'S SAFETY NET – a method for catering for three different communication needs (from Room To Develop)	Chapter 2
PRIME MOVERS & DEDICATED AMBASSADORS – a process for combining leadership strengths to compensate for individual weaknesses (from Room To Master)	Chapter 3
THE THREE LEADERSHIP CALIBRES – a test of a manager's galvanising capability (from Room To Master)	Chapter 4
PAIRING FOR PERFORMANCE – a system of upward audit (from Room To Master)	Chapter 5
SEEDS - a feedback framework (from Room To Master)	Chapter 5
THE NERVE-JUDGEMENT TOOL – an influencer's behavioural model (from Room To Master)	Chapter 5
PLUS 3 – a coaching system (from Room To Develop)	Chapter 6
THE BALANCING ACT – a model for high performing teams (from Room To Excel)	Chapter 7
HIAS – a technique for high performing teams (from Room To Excel)	Chapter 7
4X = HPT – a model for high performing teams (Room To Excel)	Chapter 7
THREE PERSPECTIVES – a stocktaking system (Room To Breathe)	Chapter 8
RICH THINKING – a model for identifying allies (Room To Master)	Chapter 8
THE SEVEN MIRRORS – a stocktaking system (Room To Breathe)	Chapter 8

INDEX